THE GOLD OF THE ORTIZ MOUNTAINS

A Story of New Mexico
and the
West's First Major Gold Rush

William Baxter

Lone Butte Press
Santa Fe, New Mexico
2004

Lone Butte Press
32 South Fork Extended
Santa Fe, NM 87508

© 2004 William Baxter

All rights reserved

Cover photograph Patrick Allen Mohn © 2004

ISBN 0-9666860-3-9   (pbk.)

Library of Congress Control Number: 2004090356

Printed in the United States of America

Contents

Gold in the Mountains 1
    Indians, geology, the lure of gold

Dolores Jalomo 8
    La mina del Santo Niño, placers and lodes

Early New Mexico Mining 14
    What was being dug in the Spanish colony of the north?

Ortiz Gold 20
    The camp of *Oro*, or gold is truly where you find it

The Santa Fe Trail 27
    The Republic of Mexico and the Americans, life in the camp

José Francisco Ortiz 35
    Real de Dolores, los ricos, y la mina Santa Rosalia

New Mexico Territory 61
    The end of one era, the beginning of another

The New Mexico Mining Company 64
    Stolen land and corporate wealth

The Civil War 81
    The War, postwar prosperity, and the Ortiz railroad

Stephen B. Elkins 102
    The Company's new and powerful Godfather

Thomas Edison 117
    The Wizard tries his hand at it

The Twentieth Century 124
    A time of neglect

Gold Fields and LAC 131
    Industrial mining, the Friends of Santa Fe County

O. M. E. P. 138
    The Santa Fe Botanical Garden and the Preserve

Acknowledgments 140

Sources 141

Index 148

Gold in the Mountains

The history of New Mexico mining and of the Ortiz Mountains is a tale of human greed and survival, of politics and murder, of dreamers and those who live off them. But it's mostly a tale of lust for that soft and nearly useless metal that has so regularly tested the mettle of mankind. What follows is the true saga of the Ortiz Mountains and the gold that was once there ...

... and the gold that is still there.

The earliest records of gold mining in the Ortiz Mountains are at best fragmentary. For over 10,000 years* Native Americans lived, farmed and hunted in and around these mountains. They probably found small bits of soft yellow stone, although there is not a lot of good evidence of this.

The very large Classic Period (A.D. 1320-1680) pueblos of San Lázaro and Blanco lie six and seven miles east of Dolores, San Marcos is eight miles north-northeast, and several other very large pueblos are in the vicinity. At any given time during the 200 years before the arrival of Coronado there were likely many thousands of people living within a dozen miles of the future location of el Real de Dolores. Some resided at the site itself.[64] It is clear from the archaeological evidence that many people were in these mountains for many centuries before the gold rush of the 1820s, but until the discovery of gold their numbers were not great and their impact upon the land was small. Most of what we see in the Ortiz Mountains today is the mark of the nineteenth and twentieth century gold seekers, and most of what we know is their story. And because the First People did not share the European obsession for gold, most of this history of gold is the story of the Europeans. Yet the larger history, here untold, must be a story of American Indians.

When the first Europeans arrived in 1540 they were convinced that the local Indians knew what gold was, and could differentiate it from other substances.[50] Indeed, the Indians of the Great River of the North knew gold, but for them it was not an obsession.

---

* A. Helene Warren has identified a Llano Culture (Clovis Complex, 11,500 to 11,000 years before present) lithic scatter at a rock shelter nine miles northwest of Dolores.

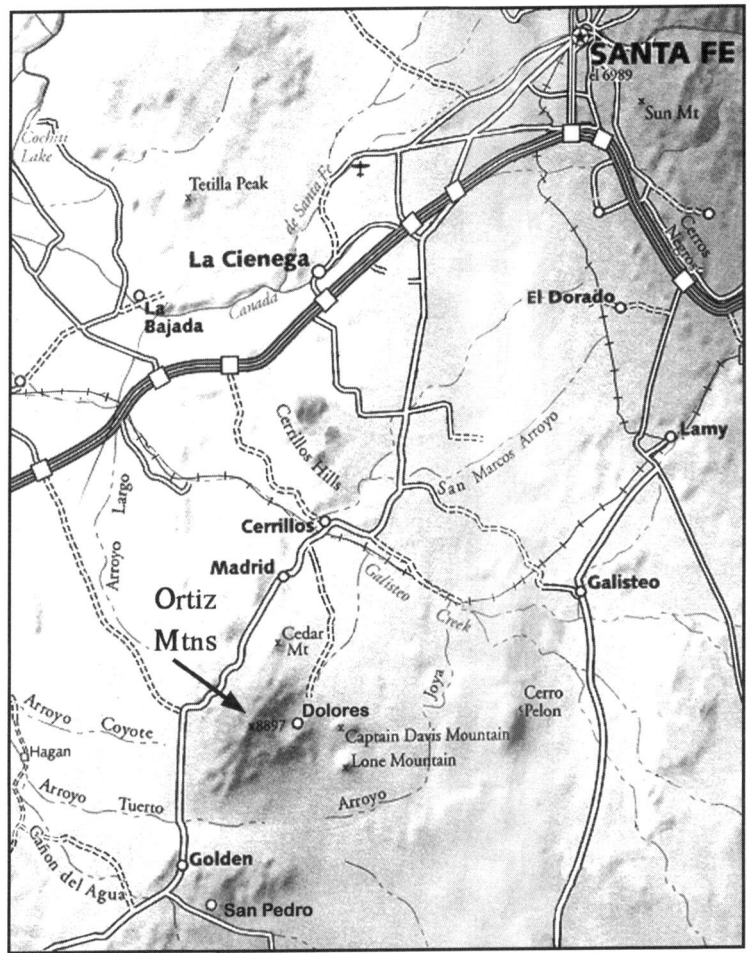

The Ortiz Mountains, with outliers Cedar, Captain Davis, and Lone Mountains. Dolores is 28 miles south-southwest of the Santa Fe plaza. San Pedro, at the bottom of the map, became in later years the center of the New Placer district. Both Dolores and San Pedro were abandoned by the early 20th century.

Of Coronado's meeting with the Towas of Pecos, John Kessell has written, "Testing the canny Indian, Spaniards had presented him with utensils made of tin. He smelled them and pronounced them neither gold nor silver, for he knew those metals well..." [30]

We have some references and hints of gold washing in the Ortiz Mountains during the Spanish Colonial

Period, 1598 to 1821, but indications are that it was incidental at most and of no real significance. As you will see, the story of gold in the Ortiz really begins in 1821, with the creation of the Republic of Mexico and opening of the Santa Fe Trail.

The suggestion that there was little mining during Spanish times is supported by a passage in a letter written by Vicar Santiago Roybal of Santa Fe to his counterpart in New Orleans in the 1740s, in which he attempted to lure Louisiana traders to Santa Fe. The Vicar tells them of the profits to be made in New Mexico: "because we are not farther away than 200 leagues from a very rich mine, abounding in silver, called Chihuahua, where the inhabitants of this country often go to trade." [30] The best inducement the Vicar could offer to the French was the silver of Chihuahua, over 500 miles away?

The historical record is more complete for the Mexican Period, and the record is better still with the advent of the Territory of New Mexico and the era of the New Mexico Mining Company.

Geologically, the Ortiz Mountains are the product of an episode of intrusive volcanism that occurred about 29 million years ago. They are part of a range of Tertiary intrusive mountains called the Ortiz Porphyry Belt that extend from a point several miles north of Edgewood (South Mountain, Monte Largo and the San Pedros) northward to La Ciénega (Cerro Seguro and the Cerrillos Hills). The main mass of this chain of mountains is composed of a fine-grained granite-like rock, usually augite monzonite porphyry, which was formed when the molten magma, driven under pressure from deep within the earth, was injected into the softer layers of the subsurface sedimentary strata. The magma may have reached the then-surface, but not in great amounts as there are no great shields or lava flows associated with this geologic event. More likely, the volcanic activity was a series of hot gas blow-outs, called diatremes*. Beneath the surface, the thick magma cooled relatively quickly.

Intrusive, subsurface magma is properly called plutonic (as extrusive magma is volcanic). The Ortiz Mountains were certainly created by plutonic and possibly also by volcanic processes.

The Mountains were once much more massive than they are now, twice their present size or even larger. One local geologist exclaims, "Think Mount Fuji!" [10] The wind and rain of the last 28 million plus years have worn away much of the bulk of the Ortiz Mountains, exposing the interior plumbing. The materials produced by that erosion have accumulated around the bases of all of the Ortiz belt mountains in wide, gently sloping gravelly shelves known as the Espinaso Formation. When you turn off of Highway 14 and onto Goldmine Road, as you ascend the mesa you travel upon the Espinaso Formation. Most of the roadway from the Galisteo River valley to the gate of the Ortiz Mountains Educational Preserve lies upon the crumbs of the original Mount Fuji-like Ortiz volcano.

The old Dolores ranchhouse is located near the middle of the Dolores vent breccia**. There are many vestiges of the one-time plumbing of the Ortiz volcano, and the vents and veins of that geological plumbing are the ultimate sources of all the gold there.

The deposit that was the source for the Cunningham Gulch gold, where the large open pit east of the Preserve is, was in the brecciated margins of a trachyte-latite vent rock. [64]

If the breccia of a geological vent is auriferous (contains gold) then the gravel downslope from that breccia vent should be very good placer ground. Correspondingly, if you find good placer ground (and the the gold is angular and wiry, indicating it has not traveled far) you should look upslope for the source of that gold, for its mother lode. When you find a source lode, as a local

---

* Diatreme: a volcanic vent produced by a gaseous explosion.
** Breccia is a geological material composed of smaller angular stone fragments held together by a matrix. Imagine concrete made with large, sharp-edged aggregate.

resident named Luís Lovato probably did around 1830, it will often appear as twisting slices of rust-colored iron-rich porous quartz within a geological vent or along a fault line. What would eventually become known as the Old Ortiz lode was described as "distinct quartz fissure veins and stringers."[24] In Lovato's case the intertwined rusty dark brown-black and milky white quartz rock contained tiny (and occasionally not so tiny) flakes, scales, and threads of metallic gold.

Much later, in 1896, J.T. McLaughlin, talking about the geology of the placer land immediately east of Dolores, said, "On the east side of the range are large fields of rich placers – decomposed quartz in the form of sand and gravel, which have inundated most of the entire eastern slope. Here are thousands of millions of cubic yards of gold bearing material that rests on soft sandstone. These deposits were largely made in a past age, but after the mountains had uplifted and had afforded great quantities of gold bearing material which was freed by the rapid erosion of the country rock.... Just above the main eastern dyke and paralleling it for several miles, will probably be found the richest 'dry placer' deposit in the entire field."[43]

"Most placer gold deposits in New Mexico," says Maureen Johnson, "are derived from gold-bearing mineralized areas in Tertiary intrusive rocks, and occur in gravels of alluvial fans, gulches, and rivers adjacent to the source." ... "The most productive lode deposits throughout the State are the fissure veins in Tertiary intrusive rocks..." Ms. Johnson continues with specific reference to the Ortiz: "Placers are found on the eastern and southern slopes of the Ortiz Mountains; the gold occurs in both creek and mesa gravels. The richest gravels are found on the eastern slope of the mountains in the vicinity of Dolores and Cunningham Gulch; here, the gold is in mesa gravels that are the upper part of an old debris fan formed at the mouth of Cunningham Gulch. Substantial amounts of gold were also recovered from creek gravels in Dolores Gulch and Arroyo Viejo. Placers are also found on the southern slope of the mountains, north of Arroyo Tuerto, in the vicinity of Lucas Canyon; these deposits were not so rich as those found near the town of Dolores."[24]

By the early years of the nineteenth century tales of the gold of New Mexico had reached the far off United

States. Captain Meriwether Lewis proposed in a letter to President Thomas Jefferson on August 21, 1803 that he be authorized to go up the Kansas River toward Santa Fe while William Clark would take a different route to the west. Jefferson said no. "Concerned about Lewis moving into Spanish territory, with its reported gold and silver mines, Jefferson wrote back that he should not go toward Santa Fe, that his mission was to follow the Missouri River to its source and beyond." [11]

In 1820, nineteen-year-old David Meriwether, curious to see the reported precious metals being mined somewhere along the Rio Grande, came to New Mexico as part of an American trading party. Immediately upon arrival the entire party was arrested and confined in the dungeon at the west end of the Palace of the Governors in Santa Fe. A month later Meriwether and the rest of the Americans were summarily expelled from New Mexico. He had no opportunity to visit the working mines he had come so far to see. But he didn't forget them.

Thirty-four years later, on August 8, 1853, David Meriwether found himself again at the Palace of the Governors, this time to take the oath as the third civilian governor of the Territory (1853-1857). [37]

What was it that Meriwether didn't see in 1820? Even today it is difficult to say what mining was going on in 1820, and where. There were many wild rumors of gold in New Mexico, a few reliable reports, and very few documents.

Dolores Jalomo

The earliest mining document from the Ortiz Mountains bears the date of December 30, 1831, when Luís Lovato sold the smaller part of *la Mina del Santo Niño**, south of *Ojo del Oso***, to Dolores Jalomo***, who had denounced it. Jalomo was a miner who had come from the south, from the rich mining area of San Luís Potosí. Lovato sold three *varas*, or one-eighth of the claim****, to Jalomo, as well as giving him the right to work it.

> Dolores Jalomo made a claim to a virgin vein of gold that he found in the little mountain, in the Cañada of the springs of waters of gold above. The said vein faced to the east, its direction ran from west to east, as did also the mine that was in the same hill of the said vein that, by tradition, was called the gold mine in ancient times. Not knowing who was the last owner, Jalomo claimed the location for gold, silver, copper "or the metal that God shall be pleased to give me." Public notices were duly posted on the door of the little church of Oro, *Nuestra Señora de los Dolores*, notifying any heirs to the mine and vein to appear in their own behalf. The citizen Luis Lovato responded, justifying his claim as owner of the land, and agreed on December 30, 1831, to permit the petitioner to claim three varas for development.[8]

That Lovato sold one-eighth of the mine suggests that he had three other partners, and was selling half of his share to Jalomo. Or it may be that there were eight partners and Lovato was selling out all of his interest. That Lovato was still resident in Dolores seven years later, and presumably still working in the mines, argues that Lovato did not sell out. His part-

---

* The Mine of the Holy Child.
** Bear Spring.
*** Most frequently "Dolores Jalomo", but sometimes "Dolores Palomo".
**** The share of a claim was commonly given in a number of varas of the (normal) 24-vara width of the claim. Therefore three varas represent one-eighth interest in the mine. One vara was between 32 inches and 33 inches.

ners, if any, are unknown.*

La Mina del Santo Niño is the earliest documented lode gold mine in what is now the Western United States.

 La Mina del Santo Niño was a lode mine, a hole dug into the ground to extract gold-bearing rocks, rather than a placer mine, which was the working of large quantities of surface or near surface alluvial dirt and sand to separate out the tiny flakes and pieces of gold in it.

Well before 1831 there were innumerable gold placer workings on and around the Ortiz Mountains, but these early placers didn't leave large footprints, and the amount of gold obtained from each of them was probably small. Cumulatively, however, it was the placer mines that, until the late twentieth century, produced most of the Ortiz gold.

The early historical record contains scant reference to these placers. Royal taxes – the Crown's share was one fifth of all gold produced – and tithes to the Church – theoretically 10% or more – were strong incentives to keep the existence of one's gold mine out of the records. For these reasons, small placering operations – commonly one or two men – were the preferred means of extracting gold from the Ortiz, and small placers remained far and away the dominant means of gold mining until well into the Territorial era.

 Placer mining required a wide wooden bowl, called a *batea*, access to water, a strong back, and little else. Dump some gravelly sand in the bowl, pick out the larger rocks, shake the bowl so the heavier, fine material sinks, using some water to aid in the separation. Repeat, always removing the larger, less dense

---

* If Lovato had been the sole owner of the Santo Niño – the record refers to Lovato as the "owner of the land" – the usual practice would have been for him to sell half interest to Jalomo, or perhaps a quarter interest.

stones, and sloughing the lighter silt and sand over the lip of the *batea*. Eventually, if you are lucky, you may see in the last dregs of sandy dirt at the bottom of the bowl some tiny flecks of yellow metal. If you are very lucky there might be a nugget the size of a chili seed in your *batea*.

If you were of a more methodical nature you might spend the day up on the mountainside accumulating the sandy concentrate, which you would later take down to the spring for washing. If you had a dollop of quicksilver you could use it to recover all those tiny bits of flour gold from your concentrate. Quicksilver (liquid mercury metal) has a natural affinity for gold, with which it forms a soft silvery amalgam. Mix a little quicksilver in with the concentrate and it sucks up all the gold dust. But who could afford quicksilver? Only *los ricos*, the wealthy.

In lode mining, on the other hand, down in the shaft gold-bearing stones were broken free of the country rock by means of the *barra* [a hard-pointed iron digging tool or gad], the *cuña* [a hard-edged iron wedge weighing a pound or two], and the *pica* [an iron hammer of 8 to 12 pounds]. The ore rubble would then be carried to the surface in *tanates** [rawhide buckets] and dumped at the *echadero* [flat place near the mine where the good ore was thrown, later to be handsorted and weighed]. The best pieces were taken to the *arrastra* for crushing, and the resulting material might then be transferred to the *patio* or shed where the actual washing or amalgamation processing took place. For smaller operations or for efficiency the processing was performed on the floor of the same *arrastra* that was used for the crushing. For this reason *arrastras* were frequently situated near sources of water.

The hybrid technique of "deep placering" appears to have been first developed in the Ortiz placers sometime between 1821 and 1840. "Deep placering", which was neither hard-rock lode mining nor surface gravel placer mining, was a means of getting to the richest placer soils, found at bedrock, often 30 or 40 feet or more below the surface. Gold, being dense, tends to accumulate in the highest concentrations at the very lowest levels of alluvial soils. A shaft was sunk into the earth to the level of the richest

---

* From the Nahuatl (the Indian language of central Mexico) word *tanatl*, scrotum.

placer material, called *pepena*, and tunnels were driven laterally in pursuit of it. In a smaller deep placer mine the miner would climb up notched logs [*escaleras**] carrying the bags of sand and gravel on his back or atop his head.

In the larger, more sophisticated deep placers of the Ortiz Mountains the *pepena* was hoisted to the surface with a hand windlass. Once on the surface the *pepena* was treated by normal placer processes.

The technique of deep placering may have begun in the Ortiz placers, but it was much more widely employed several miles to the south in the New Placer, which rose to dominance after 1839.

The record says Dolores Jalomo had denounced the *mina*, by which he was saying the previous owner had abandoned it and was no longer working it. By the law of the Empire of Spain all minerals were the property of the King (hence the use of the term "Real", Royal, to designate a mining camp), and permission to extract minerals was given to a miner in return for payment of the Royal Fifth. By Spanish King Carlos III's 1783 *Ordenanzas de Minería*, which were valid in New Spain

---

* The *escalera* logs, which are a feature of early Indian Pueblos, had been in use by Spanish miners in the lead and silver mines of the nearby Cerrillos Hills for possibly the previous 200 years.

until 1821 and continued in use in the Republic of Mexico until 1884, a noncompliant mining claim or a claim idle for a period of time – commonly three months for a lode mine, but sometimes as little as three days for a placer mine – was susceptible to being denounced, or taken over by someone who was willing to resume working it for the benefit of the King.

Dolores Jalomo denounced what he called the *Santo Niño* some time prior to December 30, 1831, and when a man claiming to be the owner made himself known, a deal was struck between them. By this earliest of all Ortiz mining documents Luís Lovato sold Dolores Jalomo part interest in the lode mine.

There might have been an earlier owner than Lovato or additional partners, and we don't know whether Lovato or the earlier or other owners called the place "*la Mina del Santo Niño*". As mentioned above, it is the earliest known gold lode mine in the West, but it is, in fact, older than we know. The mine could have been in existence for months or years before Jalomo denounced it.

At the time of the *Santo Niño* deal the little hamlet in the Ortiz Mountains called *Oro**, adjacent to Oso Springs, had been in existence for perhaps ten years. Why were people living there? They had their simple, sometimes crude houses, worked their gardens and tended their livestock, but a large part of the answer, doubtless, lies in the name of the village.

The *Santo Niño* mine is immediately uphill from the parking lot of the Ortiz Mountains Educational Preserve. The important *Tunia* shaft of the *Santo Niño* mine now has a bat cupola over it

---

* Gold.

for the benefit of a colony of Townsend's big-eared bats. The "coyote* shafts"[42] immediately north of the bat cupola had caved in, creating by the late 20th century a gaping and hazardous cavity. In 2002, under the direction of the New Mexico Abandoned Mine Land Bureau, that cavity was sealed with a polyurethane foam plug and its surface was restored and planted. Another lesser *Santo Niño* excavation about 300 feet to the north is now fenced.

2003: the new stairway to the bat cupola over the *Santo Niño* shaft.
Photo courtesy T.& P. Brown

---

* Coyote was a term still current in the nineteenth century for people of New Mexico Indian and Spanish mixed blood. The implication was that their diggings were crude.

Early New Mexico Mining

Gold is present everywhere in the earth's crust, even in the water we drink, but almost everywhere its concentration is so low as to be unnoticed and not worth the labor or capital required for extraction. Occasionally an accumulation of gold is of such concentration that it pays for that labor, and even less frequently it brings the miner some wealth.

It is the nature of humans that they talk optimistically about an undeveloped and unproven lode, and to promote it as a sure bonanza, while those few deposits known or thought to be truly rich are held in great secrecy. As long as man has quested for the yellow metal, the rumors, reports, exaggerations and lies about the deposits, lodes, placers, and nuggets have been the norm. In this, New Mexico was no different.

Reports of new mineral deposits in New Mexico were common. Deposits that proved to be real and sustainable were rare. Occasionally the reports verged on the preposterous.

A group of men, possibly sincere men, in April of 1866 filed a claim for a diamond mine not far from the Plaza in Santa Fe. [52][Book A, p.100] The diamonds didn't "pan out" – perhaps the men mistook bits of quartz or mica – but the claim attracted for a while the attention of some of the men with money... and many of the men without.

Forty years later, in 1906, Professor Fayette A. Jones of the New Mexico School of Mines, in a piece meant to promote immigration into New Mexico, wrote that diamonds, emeralds, and sapphires were all to be found in Santa Fe County.[31]

The historical record is sprinkled with tantalizing references to discoveries of possible gold and silver bonanzas. The first Europeans to come to New Mexico in the Coronado *Entrada* of 1540-42 were singularly unsuccessful at locating the *El Dorado* they sought, but the second *Entrada* in 1581, led by Captain Chamuscado and Fray Agustín Rodriguez, identified several lead-silver deposits in the Cerrillos Hills that had been long worked by local Indians.* When in 1598 Juan de Oñate established the first European colony in New Mexico, Felipe de Escalante was with him. Escalante was a miner who had participated in the Chamuscado expedition and had previously explored the Cerrillos Hills (at that time known as *Sierra de San Marcos*) area, and in one reference Oñate calls the Cerrillos mines *las minas de Escalante*.

Vicente de Zaldivar, Oñate's nephew and right-hand man, stated in 1600 that it was he who had discovered the Cerrillos Hills mines. Zaldivar received directions from Oñate in 1600 leading to the construction somewhere in the vicinity of modern Cerrillos or Golden of what may have been the first New Mexico ore processing mill, probably for silver.[20]

> Carroll Riley places Zaldivar's mill near modern Golden, on the south side of the Ortiz Mountains. On March 5, 1599, in a letter to Viceroy Monterrey, New Mexico Governor Juan de Oñate "...asked that the viceroy send irons with the royal stamp to mark the silver ingots. Oñate continued to tout the silver mines

---

* Lead glaze decorated ceramics (pottery) first appeared among the Northern Rio Grande Pueblos in the 1320s, and quickly became enormously popular and were widely manufactured. Some galena (lead ore) lodes in the Cerrillos Hills have been specifically identified as a major source of that lead. There is no evidence, however, that the fourteenth- and fifteenth-century Indians separated silver or other components from that ore. The Puebloans ceased the production of lead glaze decorated ceramics by around 1700.

of New Mexico and was said to have actually constructed an ore crusher at a pueblo called *El Tuerto*. This town was described as 6 leagues from San Marcos in the Galisteo country, and 7 leagues from the first pueblo of the Salinas – that is, the Tompiro group. Perhaps it was one of the Tiwa-speaking towns east of the Sandias. Possibly it was the San Buenaventura, where Juan Martinez de Montoya reported mines in 1607 or 1608. There is no evidence that any silver, stamped or otherwise, ever reached Mexico from mines discovered by Oñate..." [51]

Fray Juan de Prada reported on New Mexico in 1638: "mines of gold and silver are not lacking... but to the present no mine has been worked there because of the unfitness and poverty not only of the Indians but also of the Spaniards." [19]

A Spanish mining camp named *El Real de los Cerrillos* was founded north of the Cerrillos Hills in 1695, with Alfonso Rael de Aguilar as *alcalde*, but Indian-Spanish conflict caused it to be abandoned the following year.

Early in 1711 Govenor Peñuela, who had sent to Parral for 30 dozen "Madrid knives" to be used as payment to local Indians for work rebuilding the Palace of the Governors, learned that the caravan had been attacked by Suma Indians and the knives were lost. Unable to acquire any iron elsewhere, Peñuela ordered some iron bars intended for use in the mines broken up, as well as plowshares for the presidio's fields. A great quantity of awls were produced and the governor gave two to each Indian. [29] Someone (the governor?) had previously gone to the trouble and expense to import those iron bars for use in area lode mining.

In 1713 the same* Captain Alphonso Rael de Aguilar denounced and registered a mine named *Nuestra*

---

* Alfonso (1695) and Alphonso (1713) Rael de Aguilar are same person - spelling was less important in the old days).

Señora de los Reyes de Linares, in the San Lázaro (San Pedro) or El Tuerto Mountains near the modern town of Golden, that he knew had been worked and filled up. (This *mina* may have dated back over a hundred years to Zaldivar's time.) Aguilar registered it for gold, silver, copper, and anything else it might produce. [68]
[WPATSA #739] Another document shows that in the next year a portion of the same *Nuestra Señora de los Reyes de Linares* Mine Grant was sold. These mines in the San Pedro area were a precursor to what was to come in 1839.

In 1714 Governor Flores issued an order for the disarming of the Pueblos, and in his order the announced penalty for a mestizo or mulatto caught in violation was 200 lashes and two years labor on an ore crusher. [29] At least one ore crusher must have been at the Governor's disposal and in reasonably regular operation. It can be further inferred that working on an ore crusher was punishing labor.

That diverse mining was in progress in northern New Mexico is further supported by the following. On August 23, 1714 in a hearing before Governor Flores it was recommended that two large Faraon Apaches captured for murder be chained to a mine ore crusher to prevent their escape. ["... *los dos Indios Grandes llenados a Un mortero de minas los tengan Conprisiones por razon que no agan fuga...*"* [66]] Homer Milford suggests the *mortero de minas* was a large *arrastra* stone and that it was in Santa Fe, since the Indians would not have been shackled like that out in the open close to their homeland**. Therefore, the *arrastra* must have been in Santa Fe where it could be watched. [42] If there was an arrastra stone or any other heavy ore crusher in Santa Fe, then there was probably ore being

---
* SANM II, microfilm R.4, f.1088, Twitchell No. 210.
** Sandía Mountain

mined nearby.*

There are several reports from this era of rich areas found in New Mexico where no mining was done, sometimes because the quality of the minerals was too poor to justify it. Brigadier Don Pedro de Rivera, reported that in 1725 no mines in New Mexico had been worked. He stated, "Some minerals, as well as copper, have been found in that jurisdiction whose metals have only been subjected to the standards of alchemy. Since they have not been worth what it would take to work them, they have been abandoned." [4]

Fray Damian Martínez reported in Morfi (1782) [59] that between 1749 and 1752 placer gold mining had taken place. It is likely this was on or near the Galisteo River. No other reference to this spate of mining has been discovered, which implies it was not an especially productive one.

Gold in New Mexico is often conspicuous by its absence. New Mexico Governor Chacón sent a report on the status of the colony, dated August 28, 1803, to the *consulado* of Vera Cruz. In the portion of the report where he gives a comprehensive review of all the minerals of New Mexico – note the range and detail of the minerals covered – there is not the slightest mention of gold.

> "At different points in the Province have been found deposits of minerals such as silver, lead, tin, and copper. The last is very abundant and seems to be of a rich grade. There is also another copper, less fine, that is blue and green, which can serve as paint, but it is not utilized. For the smelting of said metals, there is also much coal of the best qualtiy, which I believe is not common in all of New Spain. And in case silver should ever be smelted by

---

* Alphonso Rael de Aguilar's son of the same name was apparently in charge of the ore crusher in question. Homer Milford suggests that dad may have managed the mines and the son may have run the arrastra. [42]

means of the mercury process, there will be found nearby copious salt deposits, that being one of the principal ingredients of said operation. Of alum, jet, and ochre, which are easily found in great abundance, no use is made on account of there being no one to identify and take possession of it... Mica or gypsum (*yeso*) occurs, of fine quality and so transparent that in all the Province it covers windows in place of glass panes. It is also used to whitewash walls... The abundance of copper, which can be extracted with little work, offers opportunities for the occupation of coppersmith, if there were artisans of this class and someone who knew how to smelt said metal." [68][WPATSA #1161]

There was yet another report in 1822 of placer gold in the Sierra de San Lázaro (as the Ortiz and San Pedro Mountains were then known). Given what followed, this report was probably the real thing, for we know that gold in small quantities was beginning to be collected around the camp of Oro at about that time.

What was different this time was not the knowledge that gold was present. The difference this time was that there was a lot of it.

Mining with *pica* (hammer) and *cuña* (wedge), and *barra* (long bar).

Image courtesy H. Milford.

- 19 -

Ortiz Gold

David P. Staley, who has surveyed the many different stories of the first discovery of gold in the Ortiz Mountains, finds they fall into two general categories. One story has teamsters searching for lost oxen, and finding one near a spring in the mountains. When the ox dies soon thereafter they cut it open to determine the cause, and find a large nugget of gold in its stomach. The other discovery story is of a sheepherder or muleteer, while searching for a lost animal, picks up a stone and notices it contains gold.[54, 64] These different discovery tales would have more credence were it not that they were repeated so many times exactly the same way all over the West. But discoveries certainly happened in this way, probably more than once. For the gold of the Ortiz there is no confirmable story of the first discovery.

 In the Ortiz gold was commonly associated with black iron magnetite sands, called *negro** by the Spanish miners, which were prime markers of a possible deposit. These sands are commonly about 75 percent iron, and are magnetic.[5] *Negro* occurred in irregular alluvial strata between the surface and the bedrock, and those strata were sometimes as much as fifty feet thick. The gold around Oro obtained by placering was very coarse, often in the form of scales or wire, not rounded and worn, which meant the gold had not traveled far from its source.[61]

Though small-scale miners today might use a magnet to separate the magnetite from the ore, and Edison (see below) had plans to use electromagnets in the Ortiz for this same purpose, the evidence that the early Spanish or Mexican miners used natural magnetite lodestones to remove the *negro* from the mix is absent, though this remains possible.

---

* Another possible marker for gold to the Spanish was the reddish iron compound hematite, or *colorado*, which is not magnetic. *Colorado* was not a significant indicator for gold in the Ortiz Mountains.

The iron compounds of magnetite and hematite are markers for gold because they are much heavier than other sands, and when carried by water, they settled out in much the same locations as did the even heavier gold.[5]

Placer mining (including deep placering) relied on the agitation of fine earth, often in a *batea* (a prospector's pan; a wooden bowl used to wash the crushed ore or placer sand, similar to the metal gold pan of later years), so that the denser particles of gold settled and were concentrated at the bottom of the mixture. Panning worked quite efficiently when done with water. When there was no water dry placering [winnowing or sifting dry earth] had to be resorted to, a somewhat less effective process, but one that more or less worked if the soil was dry enough. Ironically perhaps, Ortiz sands were usually reported as too wet for dry placering. Until late in the Territorial Period dry placering was rarely resorted to. Almost all dry-placering in the Ortiz Mountains occurred after 1870.[42] A more efficient process, amalgamation, utilized mercury, which has an affinity for gold particles, but mercury was regulated by the government, expensive, and was never plentiful.

If the gold was imbedded in hard rocks (lode gold), those rocks had to be mined and pulverized before the gold could be separated. The crushing was usually done using *arrastras*, *tahonas*, or stamp mills. If the gold in the sand or crushed ore could be concentrated simply by gravity (water separation) and mercury, it was called "free milling". If there were amalgamation-hostile components in the ore (massive sulphides or zinc, for example), the ore was not free milling. In the Ortiz free milling gold was found above the water table. The rest had to wait for the more advanced technques that were developed in the last decade of the 19th century.

The benefaction processes employed by the Spanish were quite different for gold and silver, and often confused. The various washing, winnowing, and simple mercury amalgamation processes that served so well for free milling gold didn't work for silver. Silver in nature, unlike gold, is almost always found in compounds with other elements,* commonly sulphides and

---

* Carbonateville, the large mining camp in the Cerrillos Hills, got its name from

chlorides. The separation of silver from its compounds and mixed gold-silver from its deposits required a chemical process.

In 1554 Bartolomé de Medina, a Spanish merchant resident at the silver mining town of Pachuca in New Spain, patented* the Patio Amalgamation Process, which he had developed for extracting silver from its very common sulphide ores.[40] (The process grew out of Medina's earlier experience with copper-associated silver ores in Spain.) Medina's benefaction or refining process for silver sulphides required finely powdered ore, a large quantity of salt (NaCl), a catalyst called *magistral* (roasted copper, primarily $CuSO_4$), and finally quicksilver (*azogue* or mercury), which functioned as the amalgamating medium. All the ingredients were well mixed – the mixing was usually accomplished by walking mules repeatedly over and around the ingredients – in a watery solution (called *masa*, or mud), which was allowed to dry (in dryer climates in an open air patio, hence the name of the process), and then the sequence was repeated. After many wet-dry cycles, the number determined by the experience of the amalgamator, the mercury-silver-gold amalgam was squeezed out of the *masa*. The amalgam was placed in a retort where the mercury was boiled off and recondensed for later reuse. The remaining metalic button was usually nearly pure argentum, or silver-gold. The Patio Amalgamation Process vastly increased the yield from silver mines, and vastly increased the wealth of the Empire of Spain.

From the first years of the 17th century the complex Patio Amalgamation Process was utilized at the silver mines of the Cerrillos Hills. Zaldivar's A.D. 1600 first processing mill in New Mexico probably used this process. But the 19th century placer and lode gold mines of the Ortiz Mountains (up until the new technologies of the 20th century) relied on various forms of gravity separation and simple mercury amalgamation.

Medina's Patio (silver) Amalgamation Process had no utility for the processing of free-milling gold in the Ortiz Mountains.

(cont. from previous page) a reputed deposit of silver carbonate.
* Medina's patent document issued by the Viceroy of New Spain carries the date December 28, 1555, but as the practice of the time was that the next year began on December 26th of every year, by the modern calendar that patent date should read December 28, 1554. Personally, Medina realized very little from his patent that so enriched Spain and the empire. He eventually donated it to the Church.

The Spanish rarely used Indian names for places or features. They often initially identified mountains by the Spanish name of the nearest Indian Pueblo. So, for example, the earliest records refer to the mountains we now know as the Cerrillos Hills, with the Pueblo of San Marcos nearby, as the "Sierra de San Marcos". Similarly, the Ortiz and San Pedro Mountains were the "Sierra de San Lázaro", after the Tanoan Pueblo of San Lázaro, which was at their northeastern base. By the early 1800s the people of the Spanish/Mexican settlement of Oro in the valley in the center of the Sierra de San Lázaro, downstream from Oso Springs, were calling their mountains the Sierra del Oso (or, confusingly, after gold was discoved, Sierra del Oro).*

In the Spanish documents of this era the word "*mina*" most closely translates as the English word "mineralization". A *mina* is a location or deposit of desirable minerals, and not necessarily a working mine. *Beneficio*** or *mojonera**** were words to denote the excavation. In modern usage, however, *mina* has come to mean the actual hole in the ground.

The settlement of Oro was itself, in the next decade, to be given another name, the name by which we know it today; *El Real de los Dolores*, "The Royal Mining Camp of the Sorrows". The name comes from the patron saint of the village church, *Nuestra Señora de los Dolores*, Our Lady of the Sorrows, not from a particular demeanor associated with miners. In its short form it was just plain Dolores. The town of Dolores

---

    *   In this era all documents were handwritten, and as such the words *oso* and *oro* are sometimes impossible to differentiate. Both names were in use.
    ** Mine development.
    *** Landmark or claim.

eventually occupied about 580 acres along the drainage and terraces of the arroyo.[64]

"*Real*" designated the property of the King, in this case a mining camp.* In the Empire of Spain all minerals were the property of the King, and were thus royal. Spanish citizens were allowed to work the mines in return for payment of one fifth of their production, known as the Royal Fifth. In an effort to avoid this impost an unknowable number of New Mexico mines remained unregistered and invisible.

By the middle of the nineteenth century the San Lázaro/Oso/Oro/(later) Placer Mountains would acquire yet another name: the Ortiz Mountains.

Gertrudis Barceló, more popularly and widely known as Doña Tules, originally from Sonora but now a resident of Oro, was brought before the *alcalde* in Santa Fe in 1825 and fined for running an unlicensed gambling operation in the mining camp. Doña Tules paid the fine, and within a few years she was operating her famous establishment on Palace Avenue near the Plaza of Santa Fe. We know of La Tules' transgression primarily because of the records associated with the legal proceedings against Juan Bautista Vigil y Alarid, *Administrador de Rentas*, who was subsequently charged with pocketing part of the fine Doña Tules had paid.[66][SANM I 5:1095] If back in 1825 Vigil y Alarid had not been so venal we today might not have this, the earliest mention of the settlement of Oro.

By 1825 Oro was a very well-established mining camp with some of the predictable amenities.

---

* Compare "*El Camino Real*", the King's Road.

This famous portrait of Doña Tules scandalously *con cigarillo* was first published in Harper's Monthly Magazine, April 1854.

The Doña Tules incident happened in 1825. Go back another four years, to 1821. The Spanish had for centuries assiduously protected the northern frontier of New Spain against intrusions by the English, the French, the Russians, and most recently the Americans. They regularly arrested interlopers and shuttled them off to prison, often in Chihuahua or Mexico City. In 1807 Zebulon Pike and his party of American explorers were taken prisoner upon entering *Nuevo Mexico*, and David Meriwether had spent his time in the Santa Fe lockup for the same crime of trespass.

But by 1821 the Spanish hold on New Spain was disintegrating. In July of that year the last Viceroy, Juan O'Donojú, arrived in the City of Mexico. On August 24 he signed the Treaty of Córdova. By September New Spain was no more. The borderland colony of *Nuevo Mexico* was now a part of the newly independent Republic of Mexico.

It is important to note that if you were Hispanic and lived in New Mexico in August of 1821, we, a century or more later, refer to you as Spanish. (There were at the time in common use a great many terms which identified all the subtleties of a person's racial mixture and heritage, *Españole* - a person born in Spain of Iberian parents - being only one of these. [See footnote on page 13.]) If you were still living there in the next month, September of 1821, we today would designate you 'Mexican'. You didn't change. Your family, house, language, culture, and surroundings didn't change. It was the central political regime that changed, and in the remote regions the effect of that was not immediate. It was, however, a real change. ¡Viva la Republica!

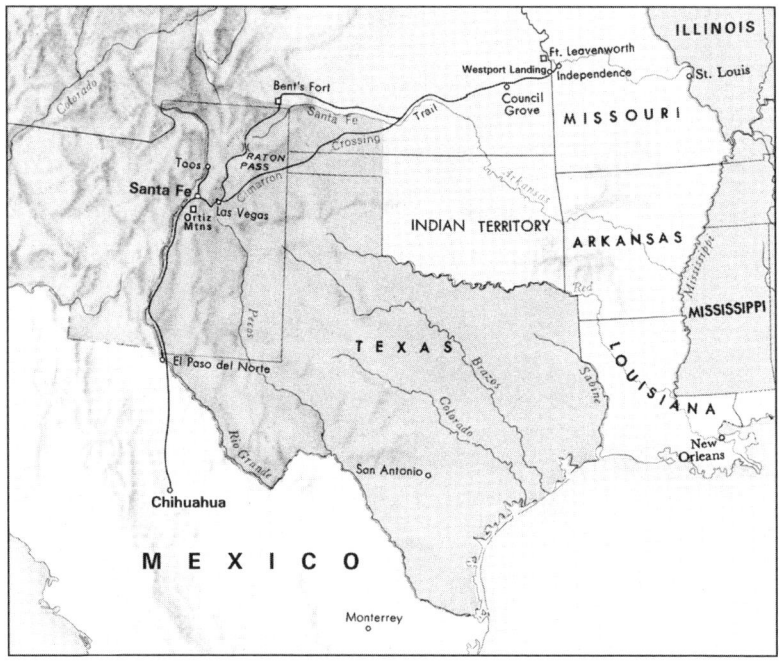

Early-mid-19th century borderlands. Chihuahua, the nearest city larger than Santa Fe and directly on *el Camino Real* between Santa Fe and Mexico City, is a natural trading entrepôt. But the Americans are coming! The year of 1821 saw the births of the Republic of Mexico, the Santa Fe Trail, and the state of Missouri. Texas joined the American Union in 1845, leading to war the following year.

The Santa Fe Trail

In the States there was news of rebellion in New Spain. A party of Americans led by Captain William Becknell, "a company of men destined to the westward for the purpose of trading for Horses and Mules, and catching wild animals of every description", [21] set out on September first from Franklin, Missouri with a pack train laden with trade goods. Some people they met along the way convinced them to try trading at Santa Fe.

When the Americans arrived in Santa Fe eighty-eight days later they found a warm welcome, and they learned for the first time of the new Mexican Republic. Becknell's company immediately sold all the goods they had brought and realized a great profit in Spanish blankets, specie – an eyewitness reported great numbers of silver dollars (pesos) – mules, and burros. [11] "If we believe Becknell, soldiers and citizens of Santa Fe who had evidently stashed away coins gave them gladly for his American merchandise." [30] Unlike New Spain, the Republic of Mexico welcomed the American traders. The Santa Fe Trail was born.

About two weeks later a second American pack train arrived, led by John McKnight and Thomas James. The McKnight-James party was unable to sell all of its trade goods in Santa Fe because of the scarcity of money. Declining to go on to Sonora, where specie was rumored to be more plentiful, in early 1822 they wholesaled their remaining goods to a Santa Fe merchant for $1,000 and 83 horses and mules. [11]

Becknell's second trip to Santa Fe in 1822, made with the guidance and assistance of Jedediah Smith, also included a novelty: three wagons. The wagons were able to carry much more merchandise than pack animals. Becknell and his twenty fellow traders' $3,000 in goods returned them a reported 2,000% profit (which equates to an extraordinary $60,000). The wagons, which had cost about $150 each in Missouri, were sold in Santa Fe for $750,[11] for a still handsome profit of merely 400%. If Becknell's first expedition absorbed so much of the available specie of Santa Fe that the McKnight-James party suffered, it must be asked where a new supply of "blankets, specie, mules, and burros" had come from? Two additional trading parties left for Santa Fe this year, and they both reported their expeditions were profitable.[11]

Compare these amounts to the balance of trade of New Mexico as reported to the Spanish Cortes in 1812 by Pedro Bautista Pino. The province imported, he said, 112,000 pesos worth of goods while it exported 60,000 pesos worth, a deficit of 52,000 pesos for the year. It was widely known that "New Mexicans lived and died in debt to Chihuahua merchants."[30] How could deficits of that scale be reconciled with American caravans, each of them taking hundreds of thousands of pesos back to Missouri? All of it did not come from Chihuahua.

The only expedition of 1823, the Stephen Cooper-Joel P. Walker party, returned to Missouri with "400 Jacks and Jennets [male donkeys and male horse-female donkey hybrids] and mules, a quantity of beaver and a considerable sum in species."[11] Some citizens of Santa Fe had managed to come up with "a considerable sum" in coin in a relatively short time.

On May 16, 1824, a very large caravan, over 80 men led again by Stephen Cooper bringing $30,000 in trade goods, left for New Mexico, and two and a half months later they arrived in Santa Fe. Though initially experiencing difficulties selling their goods because of the scarcity of money in Santa Fe (and their goods were not of the best quality), a bit over a month later they reportedly set out on the return journey with $180,000 in gold and silver and $10,000 in furs. [11] Over 500% profit.

> Much of the New Mexico-Missouri trade was limited to the small amount of cash Santa Fe merchants received in trade with Chihuahua and the south; yet an estimated $150,000 to $600,000 in silver coins, brought from Mexico to Santa Fe, was carried away each year by American merchants returning to Missouri. Gold bullion from New Mexico mines, mules, buffalo rugs, furs and wool were the principal exports, in addition to silver, taken to Missouri in the wagons. [57]

After 1831 various duties and taxes were enforced upon the American traders, both on the goods brought to Santa Fe and on the specie, gold dust, and furs exported, and the trade became less profitable, though still "a ripe plum for the intrepid". [57]

The Missouri traders made the long and hazardous journey to Santa Fe for easily transportable furs and valuable metals. While it is clear that Mexican silver coins were the major component by weight of the precious metal export, a substantial portion was in gold, both bullion and dust. Gold was worth 15 to 30 times silver by weight.

The gold and silver that fueled the 1820s Santa Fe Trail was being obtained from various locations, many of them in New Mexico – some placering was going on near Taos, and silver was mined in the Cerrillos Hills, for example – but at this time the Ortiz was without doubt the most significant source of gold. It was the gold of the Ortiz that paid for the American goods. And it was, after 1821, the availability of American goods and the need for the wherewithal to procure them that spurred the expansion of mining in the Ortiz Mountains.

> "[American] Traders were paid by the Mexicans in gold and silver for their merchandise – gold dust from a placer mine near Santa Fe, silver bullion from the mines of Chihuahua." [21]

David Dary notes that Americans dominated the Santa Fe Trail trade through much of the 1830s, to the point that Mexican dollars became the principal circulating currency in Missouri*. Eventually, American merchandise in Santa Fe became so plentiful and money so scarce "that traders were forced to sell their goods for what they could get." The Gregg-Smith caravan of 1834 (40 wagons and 140 men) got "$40,000 in gold, $140,000 in specie, $15,000 worth of beaver, 50 packs of buffalo robes, 12,000 pounds of wool, and 300 head of mules, valued at $10,000", [11] for a profit of approximately 100%.

We have poor records of New Mexican gold and silver mining at this time and no indication of how many people were involved, but in order to accumulate gold and silver in the amounts that passed over the Santa Fe Trail a significant portion of the population must have been at least seasonally involved in mining.

The vast majority of the population of New Mexico was not wealthy. Becknell reported that the going rate for a laborer at that time was about three dollars per month; the equivalent to ten cents a day. For that laborer an ounce of gold was the same as six months of ordinary toil. In that circumstance it is not difficult to understand the lure of the mines.

Additionally, there were not great numbers of

---

* Mexican silver dollars, pesos, contained 374 grains of silver, American silver dollars 371.25 grains, and both were accepted [11].

people in the region. The estimated total population of all of New Mexico in 1818, which at that time included El Paso, both Indians and Europeans, was only 45,000.

༺──◄o►──༻

After the irregular cloudbursts of each summer's monsoons and resulting torrents, the streambeds of the Ortiz Mountains were restocked with gold-bearing sediment. But the winters offered more constant and reliable precipitation, more useful for washing gold. And in winter children could earn a little money by melting snow with hot rocks to produce water, which was then sold to the miners. [34] Winter was also the season of little work for the indentured servants on the ranches and farms. So winter was the season for everyone to decamp to the Ortiz Mountains and wash the gravels for gold.

In her novel THE WIND LEAVES NO SHADOW, Ruth Laughlin offers a plausible version of life in Dolores placers.

> "The winter was dry, and the buscones* were only permitted to fill their jars with drinking water from the spring. All placer mining stopped until the first snow fell in January. Then Ramón built a small dam against the hillside, packed snow into it, and melted the snow with hot stones. They used the little pool of water to wash black sand, and Tules's arms ached again from swishing the batea around and around.
>
> When Ramón was in good humor he repeated the wild tales that ran through the camp like fire before wind. He told of a sheepherder on the opposite mesa who had seen the pale green fire that hovers over hidden gold. He said an old man had shown him a soiled map with the location of a lost Spanish mine; or he had talked to a vaquero who had crawled under a cliff in a storm and found he had slept on soild gold, but he could never find the cliff again. Another time a hunchback with second sight claimed

---

* Mine laborers who work for a share of the proceeds.

that the Spirit of the Mines, the Padre Mina, had told him of solid galleries of gold below the San Lázaro Mountains.

Tules learned to sew her lips together, but she knew that most of these fantastic visions came out of a bottle of mescal and peyote. Every Saturday night the cañón roared with wild, drunken men, who sweated to wash gold all week and threw it away in one riotous night. Sunday they slept in sodden dreams, and Monday they broke their backs again. They were sure that next week they would find a heavy nugget, a pocket of pure gold, or even the fabulous mother lode. A few lucky ones found enough to fatten all their hopes." [32]

Not every miner owned the claim he worked. At the deep placers and the lode mines most didn't. The fixed wages of a mineworker were small, but each miner was also entitled to a bag of ore as payment at the end of his shift.

Ore was transported out of the deep mines in bags called *mantas*.* Homer Milford relates that this "bag of ore payment" system assured that profitable mines, those with high-grade ores (of which one bag was worth something) had a good supply of labor. When mines ran out of good ore (*pepena*) they had a difficult time finding miners to work in them. Later, *pepena* drove American mine owners crazy as they considered it just highgrading**. In the late 1800s they complained about it constantly when they used Mexican mineworkers. It, however, is a very sensible tradition, and in many mines the worker's *pepena* was greater than their wages.

The practice of paying workers with *pepena* may explain the rapid shift of placer mining from the Old to the New Placer in 1839. As New Placer reportedly had more gold per cubic yard as well as larger nuggets, the

---

* Literally blankets; yucca fiber bags or gunnysacks, horse blankets, or ox hide sacks (*tanates*) used for transporting ore or rubbish, or for moving tools.
** Miners picking out (stealing) only the very best bits of ore for themselves.

salaried work force voted with their feet.

R. W. Raymond's 1870 report to Congress on Mineral Resources of the States and Territories gives a good description of the world of the placers, a world that had changed little since the 1820s.

> "Mining was then mostly done in the winter time. The men would dig holes in the drift at the foot of the mountains, pack the gravel out of these holes on their backs, and wash the gold out in wooden *batias*, (dishes of about eighteen inches in diameter) with water procured by melting the snow in round holes with heated stones.... The arroyos being dry during the greater part of the year, the miners are accustomed to haul water to the place of working in casks mounted on wheels, and drawn by donkeys, and to pour it into shallow tanks dug in the earth, called *estancas*. In these, they washed the gravel and earth by means of wooden bowls, or *bateas* or *batias*, continuing the operation until the water is so thick with mud as to be no longer serviceable. Working very slowly, and under great disadvantage, losing the fine gold, and working by no means all day long, or every day in the week, they naturally wash the richest material only, and this they seek by means of rude shafts dug in the gravel, without timbering, from the bottoms of which they burrow, as far as safety or convenience will permit, along the richest layers. The gravel thus obtained is hoisted to the surface in rawhide buckets, by means of windlasses – a modern improvement on the still more primitive method followed in these placers, when the miners climbed out upon notched sticks, bearing their burdens on their backs or heads.
>
> The layers of gravel passed through by the shafts in reaching the *mantas* [sic. *mantos**], or rich streaks, are cast aside as of no value; and the surface of a Mexican placer is covered with heaps of these "strippings" lying by the mouths of the shafts. By the *estancas* are other heaps, consisting of the tailings from the *bateas*."[48]

---

* *Manta* (f), blanket, cloth, yucca fiber bag. *Manto* (m), subsurface ore deposited in a wide horizontal layer – American Spanish.

Charles Lummis, stranded by a blizzard in Golden in December, 1884, met two miners who had been working on their placer that day.

> "You will hardly need to be told that gold-washing in winter is about the coldest work a man can do. He sits there all day in the weather, without any shelter, his hands and arms constantly in the icy water, and his exercise insufficient to keep up much animal heat. They had washed out two ounces of gold – $40 – that day, amid the flying snow. No wonder they kept at it! 'Most any man would stand 'a few' of weather for that sort of a stake."[35]

In the Ortiz Mountains there are a few springs, the best of them being in the arroyos on the north and east sides. Ojo del Oso was one of these, and doubtless the reason el Real de los Dolores was situated beneath it. A second spring, Deer Spring, was a short distance away, to the northwest. Most placering required either carrying the gold-bearing sands to the spring for washing, or carrying the water from the spring to the placer. If a placer was not well located the hard life of its operator was even harder.

The image on the type 2 New Mexico Mining Company stock certificates.
Courtesy of H. Milford

José Francisco Ortiz

The events at Oro that followed the 1831 Lovato-Jalomo transaction were no more than a series of attempts by the powerful and well connected to take over the action.

On June 5, 1832, eleven well-to-do people filed three claims for lode mines southwest of Oso Spring. (The mina de Santo Niño is southwest of Oso Spring.) Among the eleven were Roman Abreú*, José Francisco Baca y Terrus, Manuel Delgado, and José Francisco Ortiz. They attempted to claim basically everything; all of the land from the Santo Niño vein to the hills east of Dolores, excluding the claim which "...Dolores Jalomo has discovered on the same land, between the said spring and those which we have now designated."

This 1832 claim is the oldest application for a new lode gold mine that has survived in the Archives of New Mexico.

The registration process in the 1783 law required the locator to first present a statement of the claim to the territorial deputation, then post a notice on the door of the local church. Within the following ninety days, the locator had the formidable task of sinking a shaft on the claim measuring one-and-one-half varas in diameter and ten varas deep (about 4 feet in diameter by 27.5 feet deep). When the vein was ascertained by this process, one of the district deputies was required to visit the site accompanied by official witnesses to determine the physical nature of the vein. At the time of the inspection, the claim was measured and its boundaries marked by the locator. In this way the Spanish claim procedure allowed three months in which to determine the position of the vein before the claim lines were drawn.[42]

The later American claim process gave precedence to whom-

---

* Elsewhere written 'Ramón', and sometimes 'Abrue'.

ever first delineated or staked the area of the claim, and did not depend upon the ultimate location of the mineral vein itself.

In the far off colony of *Nuevo Mexico*, as remote beyond compare to Spaniards as it would later be to the Americans, the obedience to and enforcement of mining regulations were perhaps flexible beyond compare as well. Part of the reason for an inconsistent application of the law was that New Mexico never had a Mining Deputation as required by the 1783 law, and this lapse engendered certain discretionary interpretations and exceptions in the matter of mines. According to Homer Milford, it seems that Felipe IV's old *Nuevas Leyes y Ordenanzas* of 1625* were followed more often in New Mexico than the supposedly current *Ordenanzas de Minería* of 1783. Or portions of the regulations of 1625 were mixed together with parts of the 1783 *Ordenanzas de Minería* to suit political expediency.

During the 1801 mini placer-gold rush in southern New Mexico near Vicente de la Ciénaga**, the nearest local official, the *Comandante* of Janos Presidio in Chihuahua, decided to put those *minas* under the Mining Deputation of Chihuahua even though everyone knew the mines were well within New Mexico. This was done because New Mexico had no Mining Deputation.

Trinidad Barceló's*** own interpretation of regulations for the 1845 Tournier case (discussed below) was, in the very next year, not followed by him. Barceló found the later claimant, who happened to be not French, "more deserving". For being far from the seat of power, and far from the eyes of those in power, the officials of New Mexico sometimes exercised certain liberties, as Don Damaso López was about to demonstrate.

---

*   Spain had a surfeit of mining laws. Felipe IV's *Nuevas Leyes* themselves were effectively an amended reissue of Felipe II's *Ordenanzas del Nuevo Cuaderno* of 1584.
**   Modern Silver City, NM (founded 1870), the location of the first gold rush, albeit a small one, in what is now the American West.
  In 1799 gold, a 17-pound nugget, was picked up in North Carolina, but it wasn't recognized as gold until 1803. (As the story goes, it was employed as a doorstop for four years.) The news got out, and in 1804 the first gold rush in an existing state of the United States occurred in Cabarrus County, North Carolina. This 1801 New Mexico placer rush was the first gold rush in *Nuevo Mexico*, and the first gold rush on land that is now the United States.
*** Gertrudis' brother. New Mexico was a very small place.

There is no record of any action taken on the three 1832 claims of the eleven *ricos*. Whatever transpired, three claims, possibly because of their excessive acreage, were not granted.

One of the *ricos*, Manuel Delgado, was the owner of the two Cerrillos land grants, the owner of a store in Dolores, and the operator (along with others) of the minas de Tiro, Santa Rosa and Ruelena (lead-silver mines) in the Cerrillos hills. Now he was trying to get in on the Dolores gold lode mines. He was not very successful in the Ortiz Mountains, but he eventually owned what was probably the most famous gold lode mine of the Mexican and early U.S. period, which was several miles to the south in the San Pedro Mountains, *la mina Delgado*.

Manuel Salustiano Delgado
1792-1854
Artist: Ionitza
Image courtesy of Claire Hill

The second attempt to acquire the gold lode came three months later, on September 11, 1832, when Roman Abreú - the same Roman Abreú who had led the previous effort - this time denounced Jalomo's Santo Niño mine. It was barely a year earlier that Dolores Jalomo had purchased working rights to the mine from Luis Lovato, and now Abreú announced that it was abandoned. Had Jalomo truly ceased to work the Santo Niño? Whatever the case, Abreú's attempt to take over Jalomo's mine also appears to have failed, as will be evident.

An interesting sidebar in the Abreú case comes from the testimony he gave on October 29, 1832 in support of his denouncement. He said that on October 5 he had found gold nuggets at the Jalomo mine, which is interesting enough for a supposedly abandoned mine, and he further testified that the mining area was known as "Real de los Dolores". This testimony by Abreú is the first recorded use of the name el Real de los Dolores.

Real de Dolores had a population that varied significantly with the seasons. By the 1830s it was regularly as large as 3,000 during the winter when there was little for indentured servants to do at the haciendas, or workers on the farms, and when there was the maximum snow and water available in the mountains with which to wash the gravel. Three thousand people represented about one out of every sixteen people living in all of *Nuevo Mexico* at that time. For most of the Territorial Period the permanent population of Dolores hovered at around two hundred.

> A survey of the site of the village of Dolores done in 1993 detected the foundations of 68 buildings. [64] Evidently, the bulk of the wintertime population of Ortiz at this time occupied very temporary shelters.

The next assault, the third assault on the Santo Niño mine, took place on September 18, 1833 when José Francisco Ortiz and Ignacio Cano bought for 100 pesos from José de Jésus García and Rafael Alejo a certain "undeveloped gold vein". This transaction turned out to be of enormous significance. It was this 100-peso purchase of García and Alejo's undeveloped *mina* that led directly to the Ortiz Mining Grant that we know today.

José Francisco Ortiz was born into a New Mexican *rico* ranching and merchant family. By 1819 he was active in mercantile business and by 1832 he was involved in Dolores, where he may have held an alcalde-like position (*hombre bueno*). He was a lieutenant in the Santa Fe Militia Company at this time and may have commanded a contingent of militia at Dolores as well. His Dolores store had probably been established by this time.

Earlier, in 1818, Ortiz, in partnership with Francisco Ortiz and Fernando Delgado (two other merchants), obtained merchandise from Chihuahua for which repayment was to have been in *carneros* (rams) valued at 7 reales each, and the remainder in cash. The debt was never contested, but it was not repaid at the agreed time either. Most of the liability for this debt ultimately fell to the very wealthy José Francisco Ortiz, who owned five houses, a very large land grant, a ranch at Abiquiú, and had credits due to him of at least 14,000 pesos. [60] The ultimate disposition of this debt is unknown.

Damaso Lopez, whose brother was the Chihuahua creditor, traveled from Chihuahua to New Mexico specifically to collect on this debt. Damaso Lopez plays an important role in this story.

Ortiz' first known interest in a lode mine was with Roman Abreú and the 1832 failed claim mentioned above. In 1833 he bought the Santa Rosalia Mine with the merchant Ignacio Cano. They succeeded in getting a Mine Grant for the Santa Rosalia property in December 1833, but the mine was not very successful and only operated intermittently. The Santa Rosalia, however, played a pivotal role in the subsequent history of the area.

José Francisco Ortiz served in the expedition that captured the Texas invaders in 1841, and on July 16, 1846 Ortiz may have been the host at his home for the night meeting between New Mexico Governor Armijo and the American Captain Cook and their assistants, to work out the bloodless transfer of power to the

Americans. Ortiz' wife went by her own name, Maraquinta Montoya, and they had no children*. José Francisco Ortiz died in his 50s in Santa Fe on July 22, 1848. [40]

Ortiz owned perhaps the most substantial building in the town of Dolores, and Townley suggests Ortiz' main house has survived, with considerable modifications, to the present day. It is, he says, the large Ortiz Ranch Headquarters building on the west side of Dolores townsite. [61] But one 1860s map shows the Ortiz house in a different location. [42]

Ignacio Cano (sometimes Ygnacio Cano) was born in Sonora or Spain – it is unclear which. He was a merchant and resident with his family in Real de Dolores in the 1830s. He died in 1836 or 1838.

Once they had the land, Ortiz and Cano applied, on November 15, to Francisco Baca y Ortiz, the alcalde of Santa Fe, to be granted the Santa Rosalia Lode Mine Grant. Ortiz and Cano asserted that they had discovered this vein (*mina*), an important distinction, since by mining law the *descubridora*, the first claim on the *mina*, was entitled to an area equal to three regular claims,** probably 24 by 200 varas each (about 66 feet by 550 feet each) – though the final size and proportions of the claim were determined after the discovery shaft revealed the nature of the vein. All subsequent claimants could request only one claim.

The description of the Ortiz-Cano *mina*'s location matches the location of that of the eleven *ricos* from the previous year.

On December 13, following the requirements of the law, alcalde Baca y Ortiz appointed mining expert

---

* The absence of direct Ortiz heirs cannot be overlooked as a factor in the shenanigans of John Greiner some five years after José Francisco's death.
** In Canada today, unlike the United States, the first discoverer of a new deposit is legally entitled to stake a larger claim than subsequent claimants. [5]

Damaso* Lopez, and less than a week later he, in company with the alcalde, his assistant Manuel Delgado**, and the local miners Dolores Jalomo, Marcelino Abreú, and Nestor Armijo, all assembled at Real de los Dolores to inspect the Ortiz-Cano claim. What they should have found when they got to the new and "undeveloped gold vein" was Ortiz' and Cano's discovery shaft. What they found in addition on that vein were the two or more shafts of the old Mina de Santo Niño! Clearly, this mina had already been discovered, and consequently Ortiz and Cano should be entitled to only one claim.

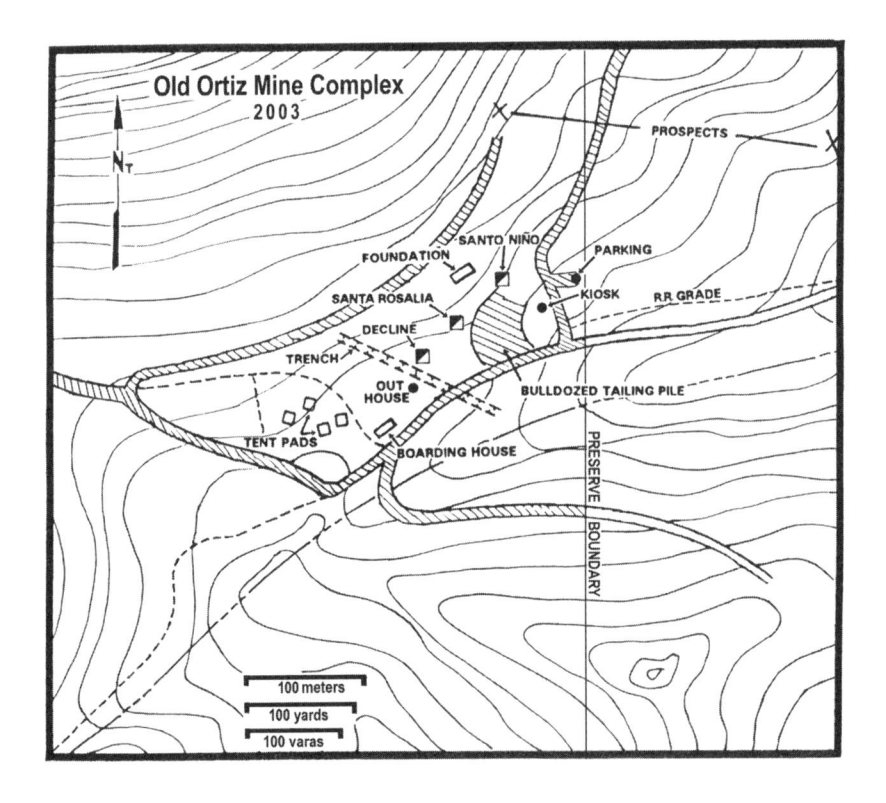

---

* Elsewhere written 'Damasio' or 'Damasco'.
** Manuel S. Delgado. See page 37.

Alcalde Baca y Ortiz quickly worked out a compromise of claim boundaries between Ortiz and Cano of the Santa Rosalia and the Santo Niño owners, and on the same day initiated a formal request for a grant for the Santo Niño. La Mina del Santo Niño was about to become legitimate in return for acquiescing to and compromising a portion of that *mina* in favor of Ortiz and Cano's Santa Rosalia.

> The modern relic of la Mina de Santa Rosalia, also known as the Old Ortiz Mine, is the shallow excavation about 700 feet south of the Santo Niño bat cupola. It is immediately north of the deep, late 20th century bulldozed trench. The original Santa Rosalia shaft is about half that distance (about 325 feet) south of the bat cupola, but it has been filled. As of this date a scrubby little peach tree marks the site of the filled-in shaft. The decline adit was dug in 1866-67 so that the new rail cars could be brought into the mine, where they were loaded with ore. A winch [see illustration on page 91], possibly a horse or mule powered whim, pulled the loaded cars, which might have weighed when loaded between one and two tons, up the decline and to the surface. From there gravity, together with judicious braking, enabled the full ore cars to roll all the way down to the mill at Dolores. On the hillside uphill from the original Ortiz shaft there are building foundations and the remnants of a reservoir that was part of a mine dewatering system of the late 1800s. The reservoir was also probably a source of water for on-site ore processing, as well as for the steam engine.
>
> The Laboratory of Anthropology of the Museum of New Mexico has assigned the Old Ortiz Mine complex the Archaeological Records Management System (ARMS) number LA 83570.

Damaso Lopez approved the Ortiz-Cano claim as a new discovery on December 18, 1833, even though the Santa Rosalia clearly was not a new discovery. This gave Ortiz and Cano three contiguous claims on the south side of the Santo Niño totalling 66 feet in width and 1650 feet in length (24 varas by 600 varas).

The Dolores Jalomo -Ygnacio Ladron de Guevara* Santo Niño single mining grant of 24 varas by 200 varas was provisionally approved on December 19th, 1833, and was given final approval the next day, December 20, after the payment of 59 pesos. The boundary between the Santa Rosalia and the Santo Niño claims was set at a point 80 varas (about 220 feet) north of the Santa Rosalia shaft.

Lopez, and ultimately alcalde Baca y Ortiz, in recognition of the Santo Niño as the earlier mine, gave preferential use (timber, pasturage, water) of the lands around the Santo Niño for one league in all directions, or four square leagues**. Lopez also gave the Santo Niño preferential use of Oso Spring, but with the covenant that Oro residents would continue to use the spring for drinking water. [65][Twitchell 1014 & 813] Lopez also ordered the Santo Niño owners to cooperate with Ortiz and Cano on the use of that spring.

The Mexican government granted usage of these large plots of land in an attempt to support any commercial development. However, the pasturage and other rights could be withdrawn at any time. They were not to be transferred along with the mine grant; and support would terminate if the mining operations ceased or proved to be barren. [61]

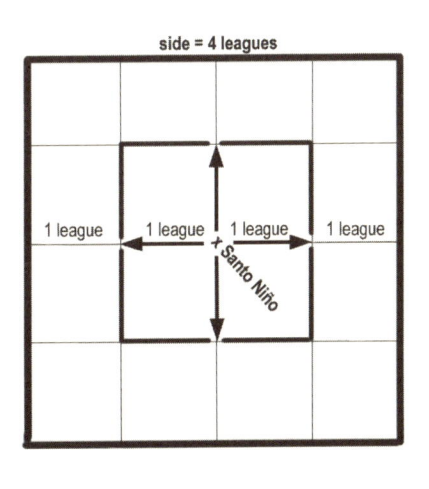

---

* By this time Luis Lovato is no longer mentioned, though there is good evidence that he continued to live in Dolores for several years.
** Sometime between 1710 and 1760 the 3.46-mile, 6,666 2/3-vara Spanish league, *legua comun*, used to measure distance traveled, had been supplanted for all purposes by the 2.604-mile, 5,000-vara Mexican league, *lega legal*, which until that time had been primarily the measure of land. Leagues in the Ortiz Mountains are 2.604 miles long.[40]

The Ortiz-Cano Santa Rosalia claim received similar pasturage, water and timber rights to a further league extending on all sides of the Santo Niño's central four square leagues, or twelve additional square leagues!

In years to come the Ortiz Mining Grant would eventually encompass the full sixteen square leagues; 69,458 acres, or a fraction over 108 square miles, and beginning in 1861 would comprise the surface as well as mineral rights for the entire property.

> The mineral rights to the Ortiz Mine Grant were not separated from the surface rights until 1948.

The "Ortiz vein" is traceable for 5,100 feet, but only these two lode claims – the Santo Niño and the Santa Rosalia – at the south end of that vein, barely over 200 feet apart, appear to have been worked prior to New Mexico's acquisition by the United States. Homer Milford reports that based on 1860 assays, with 1830's technology the ores of the Ortiz vein were profitable only from the Santo Niño's north shaft (known as the *Tunia* shaft, now covered by the bat cupola) to about a hundred feet south of the Santa Rosalia. Of these, the *Tunia* shaft contained the highest-grade ore. Thus, for all of their three claims and 1650 feet of vein, J. F. Ortiz and I. Cano held only about 326 feet of workable gold vein.

Other Mexican Period lode gold mines were operated on the east side of the Oso Springs valley, in Arroyo Viejo and around what is now known as the Cunningham deposit. The 1833 *mina del Compromiso*, known to be downstream of the Ortiz mine, was probably on the Cunningham deposit. The modern Gold Fields Limited open pit gold mine is in this area.

Soon in the new year of 1834 Jalomo and Ladron de Guevara were joined by a new and powerful partner: Marcelino Abreú. Marcelino was one of the witnesses for the Ortiz-Cano claim and the brother of ex-governor Santiago Abreú (in office 1832 to 1833). Ex-governor Santiago was now the *alcalde de Santa Fe*.

But Marcelino Abreú's partnership with Jalomo and Ladron de Guevara didn't last long. On February 19, 1834, Jalomo, Ladron de Guevara and Abreú sold 3/4 interest (18 varas) in the Santo Niño to Antonio Robidoux (Robidú) for 300 pesos outright, and the loan of a further 200 pesos*. This sale included all of Marcelino Abreú's interest. Homer Milford surmises Robidoux got one of the Santo Niño shafts, and Jalomo and Ladron de Guevara kept the other.

Later in the same year, on August 19, Jalomo sold the remainder of the Santo Niño, which was six varas worth, to Juan Damaso Salazar for 300 pesos. [55][SANM 5:304 902] With this sale Jalomo and Ladron de Guevara disappear from our story.

At about this same time Damaso Lopez, the expert who had first brokered and approved the Santa Rosalia claim, joined in a partnership with José Francisco Ortiz and Ignacio Cano. Damaso Lopez was part of an influential Chihuahuan merchant and mining family, and had come in 1820 to *el Norte* to collect the 12,000 pesos his family had advanced to the three New Mexico merchants José Francisco Ortiz**, Francisco Ortiz** and Fernando Delgado. It is not known what agreements, if any, there were between Damaso Lopez and

---

* One peso, equal to eight reales, was effectively the same as one American silver dollar, wherein two-eighths (two bits) was a quarter-dollar. A common laborer earned one-half to one real per day, where a worker in the mines might earn up to four times that, as much as 4 reales or 50-cents U.S. per day!

** Some modern sources confuse these two Ortizes – they are both members of the New Mexico elite, and both were residents of Real de Dolores, but they are different people.

José Francisco Ortiz, nor is it known whether this new partnership with the Santa Rosalia involved some kind of payback.

Lopez, who had a reputation as a mining expert, quickly assumed control of the operations of the Santa Rosalia. Josiah Gregg [16] gives Lopez credit for rapidly developing the mine, and building crushing and refining facilities (*tahonas* or *arrastras*). Townley suggests that Lopez built a series of *arrastras* at Deer Spring, immediately northwest of Dolores. These, however, were not the first, as Jalomo must have had an *arrastra* in operation for the Santo Niño at least two years earlier. [42]

The *arrastra* (derived from Latin *rastrum*, "a harrow", and Spanish *arrastrar*, "to drag"), also called a *molienda*, is a very low-tech yet highly effective method of pulverizing rocky ores in order to facilitate the separation of the desired metals from the matrix rock.

The arrastra consists of a circular pavement of flat stones, commonly three to ten feet in diameter, a vertical pole at the center, and a low vertical stone wall around the outer edge. A long transverse pole is attached to the center pole, and anywhere from one to four or more heavy, large stones (*piedras de moler*, muller stones, drag stones or grindstones) are connected by short ropes or chains to this transverse pole. A mule or burro harnessed to the outer end of the transverse pole plods around the circle, dragging the large stones across the pavement of stones, crushing and grinding the chunks of ore between them.*

The gold ore in the arrastra was ground and doused with water until it became a fine slurry. Quicksilver, equivalent to or slightly more than its expected gold content, was added to the muddy mixture as the agitation continued. The compound of gold and mercury, being exceptionally dense, worked its way into the lowest cavities in the arrastra. Then... "the operator had to drain the interior by either bailing, breaching the sidewall, or opening a port near the wall's base. With the water gone, the operator shoveled the exhausted sand and slime out, leaving a mud and sand layer on the flooring stones. The operator may have carefully washed additional material out of the arrastra's interior, exposing as much of the amalgam, smeared on the floor stones and deposited between the joints, as possible. At this stage, heavy labor came into play. The operator disassembled the floor stones, if small, and washed and scraped off the amalgam, or merely scraped the amalgam off the stones if they were large. Last, the operator filled a retort with the precious [amalgam] material and heated the vessel to volatize the mercury, leaving a sponge-like mass of metal. ...Afterward, the operator rebuilt the arrastra and repeated the process with another load of ore." Approximately a full day was required to grind and amalgamate a single charge** of ore, and the cleanup, retorting of the amalgam, and rebuilding of the arrastra took as long or longer. [38]

A *tahona* or Chilean mill (or "California mill", after the place it was first used in the United States – they don't appear in New Mexico until the second half of the nineteenth century) is similar to an arrastra except that a round stone or vertical iron grinding wheel is rolled around the circular pad. Tahonas require a greater investment in construction – the round stone, the millstone, must

---

* It is suggested that arrastra floors became too smooth for effective grinding after roughly six months of use, [28] though this assertion, which may be more a function of the nature of the stones used, is strongly contested in the case of the Ortiz Mountains. [42]
** A large arrastra, such as the one pictured, could process as much as one ton of ore per charge.

be shaped and finished, and was sometimes belted with iron bands – but they have a much longer operational life than an arrastra. A tahona was sometimes used to pre-grind the ores for the arrastra. [42]

⚒ The 1554 Patio Amalgamation Process for silver required that the ore be finely powdered. Initially, that ore was crushed either by hand or by stamp mills. By the early 1700s the arrastra came into widespread use. The earliest known reference to an arrastra in New Spain is early 1700s, but their simplicity and low cost quickly made them popular. By the 1780s there were hardly any stamp mills left. Drawings of some of the big mines at this time show 40 or more arrastras. When Americans came on the scene in the 1800s all they saw in Mexico were arrastras. [42]

Arrastras replaced stamp mills because the components cost substantially less than large timbers and iron needed for stamp mills. A stamp mill cost somewhere between 500 and a 1000 pesos per stamp, and a skilled carpenter was required to construct it. An arrastra cost about 50 pesos, and "any shmuck could build it". [42] Everyone also realized that arrastras did a better job of grinding the ore than stamp mills. That is why during the peak production years after the Civil War the Ortiz Mine used arrastras at Dolores to treat ore even after it had been through the stamp mill there. The New Live Oak mine near the east boundary of the Ortiz Mountains Educational Preserve employed an arrastra into the twentieth century. [42]

As for the design and construction of the early stamp mills, we are fortunate to have detailed records from the 1580s from Potosí, and one painting. Most stamp mills in the north were powered by mules or horses. Even in Zacatecas, where there were a couple of small streams, more stamp mills were animal powered than water powered. A log was used as the hammer of the stamp, the end of it capped with iron. A stone served as the anvil.[42]

There were undoubtedly a great number of arrastras built in the Ortiz Mountains over the years, but very few of them have survived intact. An essential step in processing a charge of ore was to disassemble the arrastra in order to salvage the valuable ore or amalgam on the surfaces of the stones and in the cracks between them. With a couple of exceptions, the only evidence of an arrastra you will find today is a slab of stone with an exceptionally smooth, flat, sometimes curved-grooved surface. If there are grooves on the stone the size of the original arrastra can be computed from the radius of the flattest curves.

A five-foot diameter stone-filled iron rim was identified in early 2003 by Todd Brown a few yards south of the OMEP kiosk. This may be an intact arrastra, but as of publication date this had not been verified.

There is a tiny concrete arrastra at a claim on private property east of the Ortiz Mountains Educational Preserve, built in the early 1900s.

Ignacio Cano, the Dolores merchant and partner of José Francisco Ortiz, might have died in 1836, though some accounts say his demise was in 1838.

In the 1838 account, Ortiz and Cano sold their Santa Rosalia property in 1838 for $3,000 to Manuel Delgado and Carlos Beaubien, who paid $1,000 cash and gave a note on the remaining $2,000. The note was defaulted in 1839 (probably in favor of the rush to New Placer that year) and the title to the Santa Rosalia reverted to Ortiz and Cano.* Cano was by that time deceased, so Cano's share must have passed to his widow, Ana María del Pilar Quiroa.

As for the evidence of Cano's death in 1836, Gregg says that around 1836 José Francisco Ortiz conspired to have Damaso Lopez expelled from New Mexico as a Spaniard** so that he, alone, could control the Santa Rosalia Mining Grant. If in 1836 Lopez was Ortiz' only obstacle, then Cano had to have been gone.

However, Gregg's statement on Lopez's expulsion is probably not accurate. Lopez did leave the Santa Rosalia around this time, but he was not expelled and he did not leave New Mexico. In 1834 or thereafter, Damaso Lopez entered into a mercantile partnership with Manuel Alvarez in a store in Santa Fe. (Alvarez, a Spainard himself, escaped the expulsion order because he was the U.S. Consul in Santa Fe.) The timeline is not clear, but Damaso Lopez's new partnership with Alvarez materialized at the same general time as he was reportedly developing the Santa Rosalia, so his tenure at the Santa Rosalia may not have been a long one.

Sometime between 1840 and 1846 Lopez left the Alvarez store and became involved in the New Mexican sheep industry, which in 1849 became momentarily very lucrative because of the exorbitant prices sheep brought in the California gold country. "Damasco Lopes" is listed on the first U.S. Census of New Mexico, taken in December 1850, as a 59 year-old resident of Santa Fe, occupation not specified, born in Spain, living

---

* From testimony given in "Cano vs. New Mexico Mining Company", Santa Fe District Court Civil Case 9d, February 12, 1865.
** The Mexican National Congress had promulgated the Law of December 20, 1827, amended and reiterated in the Law of March 20, 1829, expelling persons of Spanish birth from the Republic.

with 24-year-old New Mexico-born and illiterate Juana Garcia. Lopez lists the total value of his estate at that time as $8150 (a very large sum). He died in 1852 of heatstroke, while driving a herd of sheep into California.

Whatever Lopez's participation in the Santa Rosalia, and whenever Cano actually died, José Francisco Ortiz emerged as the apparent sole owner of the Santa Rosalia Grant sometime after 1836. As such, the Santa Rosalia mine grant would become known by his name: the Ortiz Mine Grant.

Through most of the Mexican Period there were foreigners resident in Dolores – Americans, Frenchmen and Spaniards – but they were never numerous. Foreigners suffered uneven treatment at the hands of New Mexico officialdom. One of the best known and most instructive examples is the case of the murder of Andrew W. Daily.

Andrew W. Daily (Daley, or *Andrés Dele* or *Dayle* in Spanish) was a clerk in a store owned by Juan (John) Langham located in the suburb of Dolores del Oro known as *Paraje de las Norias.* Both Daily and Langham were Americans, Langham being "a long-time Santa Fe merchant" and Daily having been in New Mexico since at least 1834. On the night of February 18, 1838 Daley was murdered in the store – bludgeoned to death with stones – and some of the merchandise and money was missing. His killers, Salvador Barela y Borrego from San Juan and Diego Martín from Ojo Caliente, farmers who were concluding a winter's work in the placer, were apprehended some days later in Rio Arriba with some of the missing goods in their possession.

Upon return to Dolores they confessed before *Juez de Paz* Francisco Ortiz (the other important Ortiz – not José Francisco Ortiz) that they had indeed done the deed. They had been planning it for two weeks. Ortiz passed the results of his investigation on to the Governor, who in turn forwarded the report on to Chihuahua for a legal opinion.

Within two weeks Barela and Martín "escaped" from Dolores.

Over a year passed with no response from Chihuahua and no attempt to re-arrest the escapees. That following year the foreign community in Santa Fe loudly protested the inaction to the Governor, and in July of 1839 the two culprits, who had been living at their respective homes, were returned to the custody of the Santa Fe jail. To head off a threatened lynching there by members of the Santa Fe foreign community Governor Armijo promised them justice would be served.

The evidence was examined again, and this time Judge Ortiz sentenced Barela and Martín to be shot in front of the house where they had committed the murder. This judgment was sent to Chihuahua for approval, again with inconclusive results.

When the two were reexamined once more in 1840, the results were consigned to the same legal bureaucracy. The years 1841, 1842 and 1843 saw exchanges of documents dealing with the legal errors of the investigation, and by the middle of 1842 the prisoners, by Governor Armijo's orders, were again at liberty. By fall 1843 the case was abandoned. [44]

It is assumed that if Salvador Barela y Borrego and Diego Martín were still alive three years later when

General Kearny took possession of New Mexico for the United States, they were wise enough not to remain in the new Territory. Memories of the murder were still fresh. But the hold of the local community, the *patria chica*, on its citizens would have made leaving home for them extremely unlikely. The ultimate fates of Barela and Martín are not known.

❖

There are no known production records for either the Santa Rosalia mine (AKA the Old Ortiz mine) or the Santo Niño mine. Gregg states that peak production on the Santa Rosalia occurred under Lopez's management between 1834 and 1836, and that little production occurred after 1836.[16] Lopez, as mentioned above, had moved to Santa Fe around 1836. Ortiz himself moved to Santa Fe in 1840, leaving his nephew, Esmeregildo Sanchez, in charge of his store, and agents or lessees running the mine. Before Ortiz departed he acted to eliminate some of the competing merchants of Dolores by filing a complaint that foreigners were building in *Real de Dolores del Oro* (the settlement's name in this document) without the required permits, which he did July 3, 1839. There are no records of the action, if any, taken on this complaint.

> Jose Francisco Ortiz' substantial hacienda in Santa Fe was situated north of the Plaza, at the site on Federal Place where the Montoya Federal Building stands today.

The Puebloan turmoil in 1837 and the murder of Governor Albino Perez, together with the increased tariffs imposed that same year on American goods, resulted in 1838 seeing little traffic on the Santa Fe Trail. Dary suggests the bulk of the trading that year was conducted by Mexican traders. It revived somewhat the following year, but mostly with larger wagons, as Governor Armijo had imposed an arbitrary tariff of $500 per wagon irrespective of size or contents. In 1840 the level of trade was the lowest in 16 years. When normal levels of trade returned in 1842 about half of the traders on the Trail were Mexican and half were Anglo. [11]

The Santa Rosalia mine continued operations for about two years, until the Texan invasion of late 1841. From 1842 until 1854 (when the New Mexico Mining Company assumed control), the Santa Rosalia may have been operated irregularly and briefly by several different lessees. [61]

⚜

Gold was worth $20 per ounce at the government mint in Durango a thousand miles to the south, but was valued at only $16 per ounce in Dolores. One story is that this devaluation was started by the American traders, and caused some initial troubles, but was soon adopted by all the Dolores shopkeepers. [61] Milford suggests it was the impurity of the gold, which commonly contained small amounts of silver, that caused it to be devalued, as well as the time, trouble and taxes (one-fifth) involved in converting crude gold into hard currency. New Mexico gold found its way to Missouri, but there is no record of any in Durango. [42]

A day's labor at a placer mine normally paid 25 to 50 cents, barely covering the cost of bread, *piloncillo* (a cone of hard brown sugar), and maybe some cheese. [1, 16, 34, 67] Country-style meals served under a large tent were 25 cents. At night caterers would circulate about Dolores selling baked goods such as fritters, at 50 cents a dozen, to the "gamblers and cardsharps who abounded at El Real." [36]

Many of the people of Dolores herded sheep and

goats. In 1848 Abert was told there were 5,000 sheep in the area, and that this number was lower than normal because of recent raiding. [1]

Iron was very scarce, and consequently was a precious metal. A pound of it was worth a bushel of wheat, or 12 cents, valuable enough that iron was sometimes mined and refined locally. Tools such as shovels, picks and crowbars were made of wood tipped or edged with iron. Spoons were made of wood or antler. [36] Cooking was commonly done with earthenware pots and bowls, many of them produced by local Puebloans who traveled about the country selling them. Pottery from Santo Domingo and San Ildefonso was in good supply.

> The 1996 archaeological survey of Dolores found Puebloan pottery in fairly abundant use in Dolores, with plain utility wares coming from the nearby Pueblos to the west, while the finer, decorated pottery came predominantly from the Tewa Pueblos north of Santa Fe. [64]

The surest way to acquire a share of the wealth of the mines was by providing goods and services to the miners. Doña Tules had done this. José Francisco Ortiz had his store, or *tienda*, in Dolores, as did Sam Watrous. The prohibition on foreigners mining in Mexico pushed them into the goods and services businesses, or into becoming lease operators of mines owned by New Mexicans. [42]

Dr. Wislizenus gives this description of his visit to Dolores on July 9, 1846: "Slightly ascending from the plain for some miles, a narrow ravine between high walls of mountains suddenly opposed further advance, and about 20 houses are seen hanging on both sides of the narrow valley. This solitary place is el Real de Dolores, or, as is commonly called, old Placer. Several foreigners live here. The first one I saw was Mr. Waters [Watrous], a New Englander, but for many years a resident of this country. He received me very hospitably, and invited me to his dwelling. Some fresh skins of grizzly bears were spread out on scaffolds, the sure American rifle stood in the corner, and everything else bore the charter of the backwoodsman; but by his intelligent conversation he showed himself a man of very good sense, and as an accurate observer." [67]

> At least up to 1846 the Ortiz Mountains were host to a healthy population of grizzly bears. The last grizzly bear in New Mexico was killed in 1931.

In the fall of 1846 Samuel Watrous sold his store to another American, Richard Dallum (who later became the first United States Marshal of New Mexico), and bought part of a land grant north of Las Vegas where he took up ranching. Look on any New Mexico map and you'll find Sam Watrous there, just north of Las Vegas.

※ ◄o► ※

At the Santo Niño Antonio Robidoux was replaced by another Frenchman, Jean Baptiste Tournier. Originally from Canada and recently a resident of Tijeras, Tournier had spent the last few years mining in the Manzanos. By the early 1840s he had come the short distance north and was working the Santo Niño.

On July 28, 1845, Tournier tried to obtain formal title to the Santo Niño with the assertion that Robidoux had abandoned it in 1835. The mine was, as he put it, "entirely destroyed and demolished without shaft, timber, capstan, or any other machinery or rooms of residence or stables." [68][WPATSA#154] To bolster his chances of acquiring title he joined in partnership with

Mariano Varela of El Paso and Luís Aguilar of Chihuahua City. But on January 26, 1846, Trinidad Barceló, as the Second Constitutional Alcalde of Santa Fe and Judge of First Instance, ruled on a technicality; that the Mexican National Law of October 30, 1845 removed alcalde's rights to give mining grants and bestowed them upon the Mining Tribunal. And as there was no Mining Tribunal in New Mexico there could be no mining grants issued. Tournier and his two Mexican partners were left hanging.

But Tournier continued to work the mine.

Later in the year 1846, just before the American occupation of New Mexico, Wislizneus visited Tournier's mine and reported that it was 40 varas deep [over 100 feet] and had a 30-vara drift [an 80-foot tunnel]. Wislizneus also noted that Tournier had four arrastras in Dolores.

Tournier seems to have persevered with the Santo Niño because as late as 1858 there were still references being made to a Frenchman's mine at Dolores.

> It is probable that Jean Baptiste Tournier is the same individual recorded in California history as an "old New Mexico gold miner named Jean Baptiste Ruelle" or "Baptiste Ruelle"* who, with others from New Mexico, made the first discovery of gold in California in 1841 [42] or early 1842 near Castaic, 30 miles northeast of the Mission San Fernando Rey de España.

Initially, placering had been the preferred mining method in the Ortiz Mountains, but it was quickly

---

* Ruelle = Turner = Tournier. After Antonio Robidoux left New Mexico he relocated to this same part of California. The modern town of Rubidoux is situated between Riverside and San Bernardino.

complemented by the underground mining of lode deposits. Throughout the entire Mexican Period and into the Territorial Period small-scale placers, which required very little capital, a minimal labor force, and could more easily escape the eyes of officialdom, were in constant operation in the Ortiz Mountains. Records of these small placer mines are practically nonexistent. Lode mining, however, with its need for capital investment and some degree of organization, is better documented.

But lode mining was also more susceptible than placering to interruption by military invasions and economic downturns. People were constantly working placer mines in the Ortiz. Once the Civil War had started lode mines operated intermittently or not at all.

The San Pedro Mountains, the range to the south of the Ortiz Mountains, had certainly been scouted and worked by placer miners for years before, especially along the Arroyo del Tuerto. But these new placers did not come into mining prominence until the discoveries of 1839 at San Pedro, at which time they became known as the "New Placer", *placer nuevo*.

From 1839 onward the Ortiz mines were increasingly referred to as the "Old Placer", *placer viejo,* though the names "Oro" and "Real de Oro" were still used into the 1840s. [42] Gold production at New Placer quickly surpassed that of Old Placer.

Charles Lummis visited "The New Placers" in 1884.

> These placers are all around the mountains -- wherever the spring torrents from the cañons and ravines have washed down the debris from the mountain sides. This wash has formed great beads of boulders and gravel, covering hundreds of acres, and varying in depth, between surface and bed-rock, from 20 to 40

feet. The diggings which gave this camp its former name of "The New Placers," are situated half a mile east of town [Golden]. The Old Placers which have been worked by the [New] Mexicans for unknown generations, are on the eastern slope of the Ortiz mountains, 9 miles northeast of here. Walking through the New Placers, one sees countless well-like holes, 30 to 40 feet deep and about 4 feet square. Over each is a rude but effective windlass -- a peeled pine tree set on two forked sticks and with a stout branch left on for a crank. An inch rope of sufficient length lets down the miner into the untimbered shaft, at whose bottom he begins to "drift out" horizontally until he strikes a "pay-streak." There is gold everywhere, but not in quantities to pay for working with pick and shovel. But in these pay-streaks the gravel is rich with yellow flakes and nuggets. Particularly fat strikes are being made now, and work is humming.[35]

After the 1839 discoveries around half a dozen lode mines came into production at New Placer, but as it was at Old Placer, so it was at New Placer. It was placer mining itself, including the above-described "deep placering", and not lode mining, that dominated production.

Maureen G. Johnson characterizes New Placers in this way. "Placers are found on the north, south, and west flanks of the San Pedro Mountains; the gold is found in subangular [rounded] detritus at the foot of the mountains and has been further concentrated in creeks and gulches that cut into these gravel beds. The richest gravels were found on the north side of the mountains where the gold was recovered from gravels in branches of the Arroyo Tuerto near Golden (especially in Old Timer Creek...) and on the south side of the mountains where the gold was recovered from gravels in San Lazarus Creek..."[24]

An archaeological survey done in 1999 by the New Mexico Abandoned Mine Land Bureau of the placer field at New Placer has determined there was significant occupation in the area from the late 1700s onward.

An estimate of the total Ortiz gold production during the twenty-five years of the Mexican Period, 1821 to 1846, based on Gregg and other sources, is 25,000 to 50,000 ounces.[41] A very small portion of this came from lode mines; almost all of it was obtained from placers. For purposes of visualization, the lower estimate would be a cube of pure gold measuring about 36 inches on a side, and the larger, about 45 inches on a side. Compare this to the Gold Fields Cunningham mine, which, during the decade of the 1980s produced nearly 250,000 ounces of gold.

In Mr. Milford's words, the two Placers, *placer viejo* and *placer nuevo*, "...produced the gold that powered the New Mexico economy during most of the Mexican Period."

For the longer view, the thirty-three placer districts in New Mexico are estimated to have produced a minimum of 661,000 ounces of placer gold from 1828* to 1968.[24] So the Old and New Placer districts together accounted for about a twentieth of the total New Mexico gold production. In contrast, in Gold Fields' seven years at the Cunningham mine in the 1980s it produced an amount equal to a third of all the placer gold produced in all of New Mexico during the pevious 160 years. Gold Fields struck it rich.

The rise of New Placer in 1839 had adversely affected the population and prosperity of the town of Dolores, but leaner times were to come.

---

* The year 1828 is widely and frequently cited as the beginning of significant gold mining in the Ortiz Mountains. It is incorrect. The true beginning date is unknown, but, supported by such as the Doña Tules information and the amount of bullion exported by the Santa Fe Trail caravans, it was at least four years earlier. A good guess for the real beginning of the Ortiz gold rush is 1822.

New Mexico Territory

On May 13, 1846, the American Congress declared war on Mexico, and three months later General Kearny and the American army were camped in Santa Fe.

The presence of the American army ironically, resulted in a severe decline in activity in the Ortiz Mountains. The hard, back-breaking work of mining was not as attractive as the numerous paying jobs in Santa Fe, providing the Americans with food and services.[14] Many New Mexicans abandoned mining. Also, after the U.S. annexation of the Mexican Department of New Mexico, local miners naturally surmised that the U.S. mining law would be like the Mexican mining law, which prohibited foreigners, and so, assuming themselves now to be foreigners, to preserve their livelihood they departed.[42] Also, some of the New Mexicans remained attached to the then-twenty-five year-old Republic of Mexico, and relocated south of the new borderline. For all these reasons, when the Americans arrived the population of Dolores declined.

U.S. Army Lieutenant Abert visited Dolores on September 29, 1846, almost three months after Dr. Wislizneus had done so. In the interim the area had fallen under the control of the U.S. Army, and there were pressures to portray Mexican New Mexico as a backward and sorry place. Prior to publication Abert's report was heavily rewritten to reflect the political expediency of that moment*, and it has been quoted often. Of the settlement of Dolores the baneful version of the report said:

---

* Rafael Chacón (whose father, Jose Albino Chacón, was the alcalde in New Placer in 1846, giving out the last Mexican mine grants there) wrote in his memoirs the only Hispanic account of Mexican Era life in the placer towns. In Chacón's view it was not a bad life.[42]

> "The houses were the most miserable we had yet seen, the inhabitants the most abject picture of squalid poverty, and yet the streets of the village are indeed paved with gold. ... many miserable looking wretches, clothed in rags, with an old piece of iron to dig the earth, and some gourds or horns of the mountain goats, to wash the sand. They sit all day at work, and at evenings repair to some *tienda* or store, where they exchange their gold for bread and meat." [1]

Lieut. Abert reported that Watrous' store and home were in *Las Norias*, a third of a mile down the arroyo, north of Dolores, but said little else about him, as Sam was out hunting when he visited.

Las Norias properly means "The Waterwheels", but in this part of New Mexico the name probably referred to water wells, which may or may not have used a wheel and bucket assembly to draw the water. In 1846 and again in 1847 Las Norias' population was reported to be 200, in 20 dwellings along both sides of Dolores Gulch. It is not clear whether these numbers are for Las Norias alone, or include the town of Dolores to the south. The very existence of Las Norias and the sizable population of Las Norias suggest there was by this time insufficient water and land around Dolores.

> Twenty years later, when a 1.5-mile long railroad was built to transport ores from the Old Ortiz mine down to the processing facilities in Dolores, there were plans, and perhaps some work done, to extend that tramway another quarter mile to the mill at Las Norias.

Lt. Abert reported one arrastra in operation at Las Norias and three more in Dolores. He described Tournier's arrastra at Dolores in this manner.

> "This mill, a specimen of all the others, was of rather rude construction; it consisted of a circular pit 10 feet in diameter, and about eight inches deep; the sides and bottom lined with flat slabs of stone. In the center of this pit an axis was erected, from which

three beams projected horizontally. To the longest arm a burro was attached, to the two others large blocks of stone were attached with cords, so that their flat surfaces were dragged over the bottom of the pit.

"The ore that is here found in quartzose rock is broken into small pieces and thrown into the pit; water is also poured in, and donkey holds his monotonous round; the mixture now attains the consistency of thin mud; a couple of ounces of quick silver are thrown in; this forms an amalgam with the gold, and when the pit is cleared from the water, the amalgam is collected from the crevices between the stone slabs, it is tied up in a piece of rag or buckskin, thrown into a crucible and the mercury sublimed." [1]

Those pre-Territorial New Mexicans who assumed U.S. mining law would exclude foreigners were not far wrong, but it took almost five years before there was an official mining law for the new territory. And the law, when it came, was Spanish.

March 12, 1851, the First Territorial Assembly of New Mexico adopted the Spanish and Mexican *Ordenanzas de Minería,* originally promulgated in 1783, as the mining law of the Territory of New Mexico, which, as such, became the first Territorial mining law in the western United States. It was superseded by a national U.S. mining law in 1866, and another in 1872. That second national law, the General Mining Law of May 10, 1872, continues, with slight modifications, to govern mining in the United States today.

The New Mexico Mining Company

The official who controlled the Territorial land records hatched a plan in 1853. John Greiner, the Territorial Secretary, purchased a major interest in the Santa Rosalia mine grant from J. F. Ortiz' widow. Shortly before that he had apparently tried to acquire all or most all of the Santo Niño claim, though the details of the Santo Niño effort are lacking.*

> John Greiner first came to New Mexico in 1851 as Indian Agent, in the company of Michael Steck. He was appointed Territorial Secretary on June 28, 1852, and as such he controlled the archives and all land grant approvals until the creation of the office of Surveyor General in 1854. He functioned as acting Governor from August 30 to September 13 of 1852, prior to arrival of Governor Lane.

John Greiner revealed his plan years later, in a letter written to Elisha Whittlesey and the New Mexico Mining Company.

> "Having long had a desire to secure an interest in the celebrated placer Gold Mines, twenty-seven miles south of Santa Fe, by far the richest of any mines in the Territory, and supposed to be, by those most acquainted with them, equal to any in California, I was glad to learn that an opportunity offered of getting the control of the whole of the Placer Mountains, and at once made every effort to accomplish the object." [from The New Mexico Mining Company: Preliminary Report for the Use of the Stockholders, 1864]

The culmination of Greiner's effort was the following transaction, registered on December 26, 1853.

---

* It is probable that the New Mexico Mining Company did not use the Santo Niño Grant with the U. S. Government because they were unable to buy out all of its claim holders. They represented instead that the Santa Rosalia, which they had acquired all or most of, comprised the entire claim. [42]

"Know all men by these presents, that I, Maraquita Montoya, widow and sole heir of José Francisco Ortiz, deceased, of the county of Santa Fé, Territory of New Mexico, in consideration of the sum of one thousand one hundred dollars, to me paid by John Greiner, of the county and Territory aforesaid, the receipt whereof I do hereby acknowledge, do by these presents give, grant, bargain, sell, and convey unto the said John Greiner, his heirs and assigns, a certain parcel of land, on which is a gold mine, known by the name of Santa Rosalia, situated in the Real de Dolores, in the county of Santa Fé aforesaid; the vein of said mine traversing from north to south the mountain called Oso, and bounded and described as follows, to wit: measuring from east to west, under the said vein, 15 varas; measuring south from the mouth of the mine 80 varas, to the southern boundary of the mine formerly known by the name of Santa Niño, and now owned by said John Greiner and others ..." [PRIVATE LAND CLAIMS IN NEW MEXICO, p.59; No.3]

Fifteen varas represented about two-thirds interest in the Santa Rosalia, and this was probably all of José Francisco Ortiz' ownership share.

If the Spaniard, Damaso Lopez, had any interest in the mine he had apparently abandoned it when he left in the late 30s or early 40s to go into business in Santa Fe. Greiner's deed explained away Ignacio Cano's interest in the mine by saying he had sold it to Ortiz on September 18, 1833. Señora Montoya* had no records of Cano's supposed sale to her husband, but no one seems to have questioned this explanation. Perhaps they weren't paying attention, or perhaps they hoped no one would notice? September 18, 1833 was the date on which Ortiz and Cano together bought the original "undeveloped" claim from Garcia and Alejo!

In a different reference the N.M.M.C. says Cano sold out his share to Ortiz in 1836, and that they once had

---

* José Francisco Ortiz and Maraquita (María Inés) Montoya had no heirs. Maraquita inherited everything, which fact could only have simplified Greiner's task.

that bill of sale but had subsequently lost it. [42] Why hadn't Señora Montoya sold the entire twenty-four varas of the claim to Greiner? Most likely she knew what was rightfully hers and sold only what she owned. If Señora Montoya didn't own the last nine varas, then Cano's widow (or Delgado and Beaubien) owned them.

Maraquita Montoya could neither read nor write.

By the Treaty of Guadalupe Hidalgo the United States had solemnly agreed to honor all legitimate Spanish and Mexican land grants in the new territory. In 1854 the Office of Surveyor General was established with the task of examining land grant claims and submitting them to the U.S. House of Representatives for validation.

> The U.S. Congressional Act of July 22, 1854*, provided that unconfirmed Spanish and Mexican land grants be held in a state of reservation; thus they were closed to miners as well as to settlers, and the failure of Congress to act gave grant claimants the use of large areas of land without ownership of the same. Effectively, this prevented anyone not already occupying a potential (unconfirmed) land grant from beginning any new activity there.

Greiner, through his recent purchases, was the owner of record for the Ortiz "potential land grant" at the time of the legislation, and that same legislation closed all unconfirmed land grants to new settlers and miners. The Ortiz Mine Grant was only Greiner's until a confirmation proceeding said otherwise.

---

* The Act also reserved sections 16 and 36 in each township for the benefit of schools in the Territory, and a quantity of land equal to two townships was reserved for the establishment of a university. Subsequently sections 2 and 32 were also reserved for common schools..

In June of 1854 Territorial Secretary Greiner, having recruited some of his superiors in Washington, D.C. and some investors from his home state of Ohio, began to organize the New Mexico Mining Company.

On August 19 Greiner transferred the Santa Rosalia to Elisha Whittlesey and six others, who promptly issued articles of association as the New Mexico Mining Company. The intent was that the company would be privately held, and that after the initial injection of capital from the partners, the mine would fund its development and improvements out of its gold production. By this means the profits could then be regularly and discreetly distributed without the burden of corporate organization. [62]

> Greiner divested himself of all of his interest in the company before 1858, but he continued to work on its behalf until sometime after the Civil War.

Abraham Rencher, one of the original 1854 investors in the company, quickly expanded his stake to 2 ½ ninths (28%). Around 1855 he became the largest stockholder and the N.M.M.C. president. Rencher, an important Democratic politician, rejected offers for several appointive governmental offices, including that of Secretary of the Navy, in favor of the office of Territorial Governor of New Mexico. He served as Governor of New Mexico from November 11, 1857 to September 1, 1861. [23] Though his papers do not reveal his reasons, Rencher clearly wanted to be where he could control and assist the company in which he had such a significant investment.

> Abraham Rencher, 1798-1883, was a graduate of the University of North Carolina, class of 1822. He served three terms in the U.S. Congress as a Democrat from North Carolina and was the U.S. ambassador to Portugal in the 1840s, prior to becoming the Governor of the Territory.

Rencher, as president of the N.M.M.C., signed all the stock certificates dated between its founding in June 1854, and April 27, 1864. Collectors take note: the company's paper certificates were not printed until 1859, so circulating stock certificates of an earlier date were all signed in 1859 and backdated.

NMMC type 1 (initial) Stock Certificate - June 1855 to early 1864.
In 1859 the NMMC moved its headquarters from Santa Fe to Washington City. This certificate, number 356, was issued at Washington City.
Courtesy of Homer Milford

The New Mexico Mining Company began mining operations in 1855, with N. M. Miller assigned to develop and manage the property. Miller, who lived in Dolores, was under orders to finance the development of the property entirely from what he could produce. But he could never accumulate enough bullion to pay for the underground exploration that might justify expansion or increased production.

For want of capital for development Miller was compelled to continue operations at the Old Ortiz mine using traditional mining methods, processing about two tons of ore a day. He mined out the last of the surface ore bodies, and worked the Ortiz vein down to the water table, which was at about 165 feet. Free milling rock, uncomplicated by the presence of other metals, was found down to groundwater, but the higher quality ores were in irregular isolated pockets and chimneys. [62]

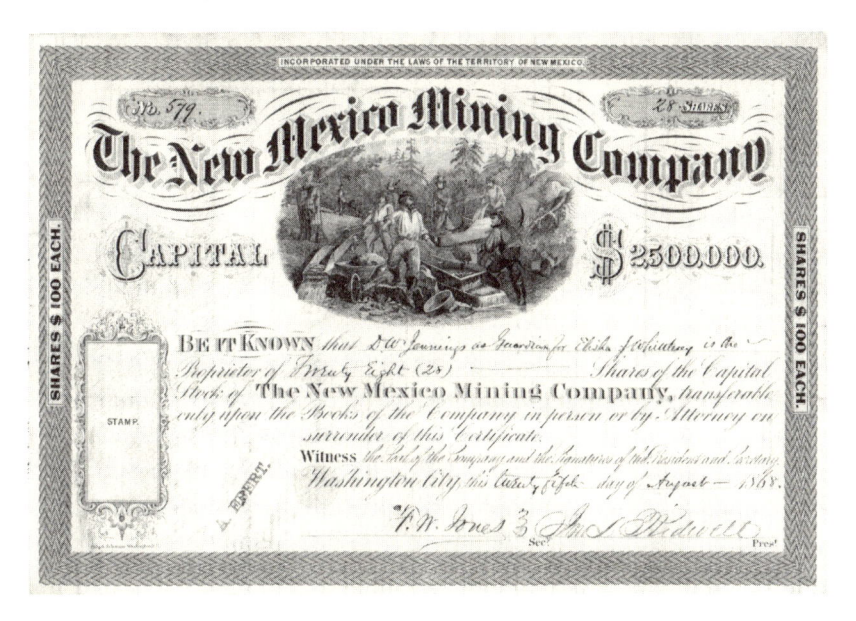

NMMC type 2 Stock Certificate - February 1864 to April 1878
On certificates issued after April 1878 "Washington City" is crossed out and "New York" written in. Stephen B. Elkins, whose office was in New York City, gained control of the NMMC in mid 1878, ending the issuance of stock certificates.
Courtesy of Bob Guzowski

N. M. Miller was probably the N.M.M.C. agent who, in an attempt to increase income, leased in 1856 some part of the mining grant to the Carondelet Company.

His tenure as N.M.M.C. manager ended in 1858, but he remained associated with the company. In 1860, when Congress officially bestowed the full Ortiz Grant upon N.M.M.C., Miller's name appeared in that document as one of six company directors.

After several years of stagnant production Rencher and Greiner determined that the solution for the N.M.M.C.'s lack of capital was the recruitment of new investors, and for this they had to re-incorporate as a public company. Greiner smoothed the process of incorporation in the Territorial Legislature by bringing many prominent New Mexico politicians into the N.M.M.C. as stockholders. [62]

As this was going on there were ominous storm clouds forming on the horizon. The various states were drifting toward what would soon be called the American Civil War, and that war would stall the schemes of the N.M.M.C., or worse. But in the meantime there was the Carondelet lease.

Juan Eugenio Leitensdorfer had been in the Santa Fe Trail trade since 1830. He had married Soledad Abreú on December 6, 1845 and was an established businessman and resident of Santa Fe. In 1856 Leitensdorfer, together with relatives from St. Louis and other persons, had formed the Carondelet Company to exploit the gold in the Ortiz Mountains. Upon acquiring the lease of the Ortiz mine, Leitensdorfer promptly ordered a five-stamp mill, a steam engine to drive it, and a quantity of other equipment, which was delivered by wagon from the States.

At least some of Leitensdorfer's equipment had arrived at Dolores and was in the process of being set up when, in August, the geologist William P. Blake paid a visit. Blake made notes on both the stamps and ants of Dolores in his August 20, 1857 journal entry, and he left some blanks he never got around to filling.

"Reached the town of Placer about 430 and passed the miserable mexican huts, following up the valley of a little creek in which the water oozed up as from springs. It is small in quantity and is carefully retained in little pools by the residents. Just above we reached the new building covering the machinery of the mill and stopped at the door of Mr. Idler's house - the Superintendent in charge. We dismounted and unsaddled. Steam engine 60 horsepower. Two boilers. Deep well for water, full – A copious supply – cold but tastes of [illegible]. A large frame building __ feet x __. It is partly roofed. Stamps - 12 - 6 for dry & 6 for wet. The bed of one [illegible] laid. Idler says 11 more to go down. Iron work for two chillian mills but no stone large enough to make the wheels or rollers. He uses mud instead of lime mortar for he cannot find good limestone near. Curious honey ants - ants with their abdomens enlarged with a [illegible] or capsule one quarter of an inch in diameter, bladder like and filled with liquid amber-like honey."

William Idler, the N.M.M.C. manager, superintended the installation of Leitendorfer's stamps and engine adjacent to the well at Oso Spring, and he constructed the building for them. The stone base or anvil for one stamp had been laid, but the others had not yet.* The two-boiler steam engine was there, but it is not clear whether it had yet been assembled. The mill building roof was still under construction. Iron for Chilean mills – large stone wheels attached to a pivot that crushed ore by rolling over it – was on site, but Idler hadn't yet found stones of sufficient size to construct the wheels. As well, Idler had had to resort to adobe rather than lime as mortar in his construction.

Stamp mills are mechanized ore crushers, functionally the same as the arrastra or tahona mentioned above. A common configuration would have anywhere from one to a dozen or more heavy vertical rods (iron-tipped logs, and later on, solid iron rods) raised by cam arms and released to fall repeatedly against an iron anvil. The ore rocks were crushed between the anvil and the hammer rod.

---

* Leitensdorfer had ordered five stamps. Blake's number does not correlate either with Steck's 1867 addition to the mill of ten new stamps, giving it a reported total of fifteen stamps (three banks of five). It is more likely that Blake miscounted the number of stamps in 1857, something he might easily have done since at the time of his visit the mill had not yet been set up.

> Arrastras are technologically simpler than stamp mills, cheaper, and may grind the ores more finely, but stamp mills are more suited for processing large volumes of ore. Zaldivar's original New Mexico mill [see page 15] was some variety of muscle-powered stamp mill, probably a single stamp. With the advent of arrastras around 1700, stamp mills fell from fashion. In the second half of the nineteenth century as steam engines became increasingly available, stamp mills, with their advantages of scale (expandability) and speed, regained their ascendency, especially at large-scale capital-driven operations such as the N.M.M.C.

This first steam-powered stamp mill in the Rocky Mountains could have been operational at Dolores sometime around August or September 1857. Colorado didn't see its first steam-powered stamp mill until 1859.

※

Abraham Rencher arrived in Santa Fe on November 11, 1857, and was immediately sworn in as governor.[23,66] In a series of letters written to his partner in the States, James Josiah Webb, Santa Fe merchant John M. Kingsbury told the Rencher story.

> November 30, 1857: "I do not fancy the Gov. [Abraham Rencher, who had arrived only 19 days before] much. He is rather on the old fogy order. He has brought a young man to superintend the mines. Idler goes in with this mail. I do not think we can calculate on anything from the mines for a year or two. The Lectensdorfer outfit will be a complete failure."[12]

By the time Kingsbury had written this Rencher had already replaced William Idler with "a young man", and Idler was returning to the United States with the outgoing mail.

> January 31, 1858: "I am not satisfied with the appearance of the [Carondelet] Mining Co. operations, don't you be induced or

persuaded into an investment there untill it is proved beyond a doubt to your satisfaction that all is right and that it is paying." [12]

February 14, 1858: "I am in receipt of yours of the 4th ult. I hope you have been able to get a satisfactory settlement of those Carondolet Notes. In case you have not, I still believe they are good and will be paid in time. Leitensdorfer has sold the whole outfit. The Engine to Hersch for $2,000.+ six months, and the balance of the machinery here & at West Port to the Gov. at cost of 15 cents freight,... It has turned out as I said a failure. They lose their time, improvements, and expenses if nothing more, which is a pretty heavy sum, and the sooner we get our amt. secured the better." [12]

As John Kingsbury had predicted, the Carondelet Company, which was insufficiently capitalized and suffered in the financial panic of 1857, did not long survive. In the winter of 1857-58 Leitensdorfer was forced to liquidate the company. The steam engine was sold to Joseph Hersh, who, holding the contract to supply the Army with flour, installed it at one of his two flour mills in Santa Fe. The Dolores steam engine was set up at the Hersh mill on the Rio Santa Fe in August 1858.

Hersh's new steam engine was the first steam powered flour mill in New Mexico. That steam powered mill continued in Hersh's hands until he lost it in May of 1879 through foreclosure. [Earl Porter, 2003]

The stamps and all Leitensdorfer's remaining equipment, including some items that had not yet been shipped from West Port, Kansas, were given to Governor Rencher in return for the shipping cost of 15 cents per pound. Leitensdorfer wanted to continue to do business in New Mexico – in fact Leitensdorfer and his family would be active in New Mexico for several more decades – so his near-donation of the spoils of the Carondelet Company to the Governor was undoubtedly calculated. Rencher later reported that he paid

$20,000 for the equipment – a gross exaggeration of the actual amount. [42]

Back to John Kingsbury's letters.

July 25, 1858: "The Gov. is still prosecuting this work at placers, but is going on very slow. I hear nothing encouraging from them. I think it is deterred much by bad management and the fear of expanding money. He is too much of an old fogy to open the mine and work it successfully. It may be that he is cramped for means which would account for the delays there. I believe he is trying to make it pay without further investment while every body can see that to make it profitable they must push the mashinery, work it night & day and spare no expense to feed it and keep it going." [12]

August 14, 1858: "As I predicted the Gov's mine with his management has turned out a failure. He has now suspended all operations there, and discharged his men. He talks now of getting Mr. Idler back again. All he has expended has been sunk. Up to the present he has realized nothing from the outfit. He is hard pushed for funds, is unable to pay for the mashinery which he bought of Leitensdorfer, and Leitensdorfer has commenced suit for it. It will come up in the next court. The overseer he had, evidently did not understand his business." [12]

November 20, 1858: "I have written you fully all I know about the Gov. mining operations at Placers. I was there myself. You done well to let it alone. I believe there is gold there. They have plenty of water and the mashinery works well but they have had no one who could separate the gold after the ore was ground up. This together with bad management has exausted all their funds in salaries and in getting ready to work and now they find they do not know how to get the gold out. I believe the Gov. has some hope of getting Mr. Idler back and if he succeeds will try it again. He has got his all vested there and it is his only show. It has nearly cost the old man his life. He has been sick nearly all the time since the mines stoped and Doc Hoan says it is nothing but nerves excitement caused by over excitement. The fear of loosing his all* is too much for the old man." [12]

---

* According to James Josiah Webb, Kingsley's partner and correspondent,

William Idler never returned, and the resolution of the Leitensdorfer suit, if there was one, is unknown. Abraham Rencher served as Territorial Governor until September 1, 1861. He died at Chapel Hill, N.C., in 1883 at 85 years of age.

On February 1, 1858, the New Mexico Mining Company, a public company, was approved by the Legislative Assembly of the Territory of New Mexico. This was the first mining corporation in the Territory of New Mexico and the first in the Rocky Mountains. The incorporators are listed as Elisha Whittlesey, Abraham Rencher, Ferdinand W. Risque, Charles E. Sherman, Andrew J. O'Bannon, Lewis S. Coryell, David Walker, Ulysses Ward, Preston Beck, Michael A. Otero, Henry Connelly, and Francis A. Cunningham. The Company was regularly organized at the prescribed first meeting of the board on January 15, 1859, at Santa Fe, New Mexico, at the Executive Office, the Governor of the Territory (Abraham Rencher) being present and presiding on the occasion.

Of these, Rencher, Beck, Otero, Connelly and Cunningham left an imprint on New Mexico. The others, although important for their support of the legislation, were merely Eastern politicians and captialists. In addition to Rencher...

Preston Beck Jr. was a Missouri businessman who relocated in New Mexico in the late 1840s. The holder of the New Mexico Preston Beck Jr. Land Grant, 38,700 acres between Anton Chico and Santa Rosa.[58] He was also involved in the manipulations of the Pecos Pueblo Land Grant. He died the result of a knife fight in Santa Fe in 1858.

(cont.) Rencher had everything he owned invested in the mines.[12]

Michael (Miguel) A. Otero, was born June 21, 1829 in Valencia, NM, and died May 30, 1882. In 1852 Otero was the private secretary to Governor Lane. In 1854 he was the New Mexico Attorney General. From March 4, 1856 to March 3, 1861 he was the Territorial Delegate (Democrat) to the U.S. Congress (he was supported by Bishop Lamy), where he pushed for the railroad. He was also partial to the South and to slavery. His son, Miguel A. "Gillie" Otero Jr, served as Governor of the Territory from 1897 to 1906.

Dr. Henry Connelly, born in 1800 in either Virginia or Kentucky. Connelly was in Santa Fe by mid 1828, and by 1830 was proprietor of a store in Chihuahua City, where he lived until sometime after 1848. In 1850, when it appeared New Mexico might join the United States as a state rather than a territory, Henry Connelly was elected as its prospective first governor. Instead, he served as a member of the New Mexico Territorial Council, and from 1853 to 1859, as the Territorial Delegate from Bernalillo. Connelly was finally appointed New Mexico Territorial Governor, replacing Abraham Rencher, and served from September 4, 1861 to July 16, 1866. Less than a month after leaving office, August 12, 1866, he died of an opium overdose.

Major Francis A. Cunningham came to New Mexico with the army, and while serving as paymaster was robbed of $36,085, but Congress cleared him of neglect and relieved him of having to pay it back. [42] In 1850, when it appeared New Mexico might join the United States as a state rather than a territory, the Legislature assembled on July 1 and elected Francis A. Cunningham as one of the two senators. Somehow, possibly through influence or investment, his name became associated with Cunningham Gulch, Cunningham Hill, and the Cunningham Deposit. The latter was the object of Gold Fields Ltd.'s efforts in the 1980s.

The Ortiz Mine claim was approved by the Surveyor-General of New Mexico, W. Wilbar, Decision No. 9, dated November 24, 1860, and this was forwarded to the U.S. House of Representatives for final action.

"...the Surveyor General, a political appointee, treated the grant as fully awarded to Ortiz in fee simple. His recommendation made no distinction between the mining claim and the grant of surface rights. The grant was treated as a single award. His survey was extended to include the full distance described in the original grant, notwithstanding the presence of private real property at Dolores and the mining claims of others who had worked in the district undisturbed in their possession since [before] 1828. In fact, the company had taken particular care since obtaining title in 1854, not to question any of the titles to land belonging to families residing at Dolores or to miners working claims within the extended borders of the grant. Until Congress had confirmed their title, no adverse action was desired through the courts. Miners continued to come and go over any of the property claimed by the company without any attempt to limit access or claim trespass." [62]

The claimants for this matter were Elisha Whittlesey, Ferdinand W. Risque, Andrew J. O. Banon*, Charles E. Sherman, N. M. Miller, and Thomas J. Walker**, and the New Mexico Mining Company. Of the primary claimants here, all were listed as original incorporators of the N.M.M.C. a year and a half earlier except N. M. Miller, whose name appears here for the first time. As well, the corporate N.M.M.C. itself is one of the present claimants. The Surveyor-General also noted the names of the original parties of the Ortiz Mine claim: José F. Ortiz and Ignatio Cano. But none of the political appointees serving in New Mexico at this time and with an interest in the N.M.M.C. were mentioned, most notably Governor Abraham Rencher. The omissions were patently devious and purposeful, intended to mislead. And they were successful.

By Special Act of Congress, Executive Document No. 28, and by the Special Act No. 48, dated March 1, 1861, the Ortiz Mine Grant, slightly more than 108 square miles, or 69,458.33 acres, was quit claimed to the New Mexico Mining Company.

---

* Andrew J. O'Bannon elsewhere.
** David Walker and Thomas J. Walker arre family.

Technically, this was the birth of the "Ortiz Mine Grant", as prior to this act the property was known variously as the Santa Rosalia claim or Santa Rosalia mine grant. But then technically, again, some time prior to 1848 the Santa Rosalia claim was vacated, becoming legally extinct, for reason of abandonment!

It was a legal error that was never repeated to consider a mining grant issued by authority of the 1783 *Ordenanzas de Minería* as a title to surface area, and thus the basis for a land grant.[42] The Ortiz Mining Grant is the only Mexican Mining Grant ever formally recognized by the United States under the Treaty of Guadalupe Hidalgo. Also, interestingly, the name of Governor Rencher, who was THE major stockholder in the company at the time, does not appear anywhere in the act. This omission almost certainly contributed to the Grant's recognition.[61]

> Surveyor-General Julian wrote in 1885: "In the case of the Ortiz mine claim, no grant was ever made. It was conceived by the Surveyor-General and midwived by the act of Congress approving it; but as that act refers to the boundaries mentioned in the papers, and thus seems to recognize them, the government has no redress."[25]

> George W. Julian, surveyor general for New Mexico, 1885-1889, tried to kill a lot of the land grants. He named S. B. Elkins, T. B. Catron and Charles H. Gildersleeve as prime culprits of land stealing in New Mexico.[42]

Julian's list of culprits could have been a lot longer. The Acting Secretary of the Interior at that time, Moses Kelly, who had on January 11, 1861, recommended to the House of Representatives that this land be given to the N.M.M.C., was at the same time the secretary of the N.M.M.C. and a stockholder in it.

Between 1854 and 1861 the N.M.M.C. managed to cover the expenses of its Ortiz operations but did not generate the profits that were expected. The 1856 Carondelet lease had not worked out and Rencher had shut down operations in the second half of 1858. But in 1859-60 the sale of new stock provided over $20,000 for improvements, including a water impoundment immediately below Oso Spring and the enlargement of two arrastras there. The stamp mill was at the same location, though it is unclear if or by what power (animal or steam) it was operating, though it was probably by another steam engine. Mining crews were expanded and there was a rise in exploration and production. [62]

About October of 1861 the N.M.M.C. leased its Ortiz mine to Samuel Ellison, a local politico* with a weakness for gambling. [12] Ellison, working a crew of 40 around the clock "near five months, when the invasion and occupation of the country by the rebel forces, compelled us to abandon the work", [13] took out "near seven thousand dollars" in gold. Ellison estimated in that same period pilferage accounted for another $7,000 in gold. The first figure is probably an exaggeration, and the second probably more so. [42]

Homer Milford points out that production of anything near the amounts claimed by Ellison could not have been accomplished with arrastras alone, which could process only about one ton of ore a day. There had to have been a functioning stamp mill at Dolores at this time, almost certainly powered by a steam engine. When and how this engine got to Dolores – since it was not the engine then in Hersh's possession – is unknown.

---

* Ellison was at different times Speaker of the New Mexico House of Representatives, a translator for and secretary to the Governor, a District Court clerk and judge, and the Territorial Librarian.

By 1862 the N.M.M.C. was driving an arrastra with their steam engine, another probable first.

In order to provide fuel (for those steam engines?), at about this time (1859) the company began shipping loads of coal from a location about four miles northwest of Dolores known as Coal Bank. For many years coal from Coal Bank had been dug irregularly and on a small scale, but now, for the first time anywhere in New Mexico, coal was being mined for industrial use. [41]

About thirty-five years later the coal mining town of Madrid was established a short distance down the arroyo, north of the original Coal Bank diggings.

The Civil War

Confederate troops from El Paso moved into New Mexico in July of 1861. When in the spring of the following year General Sibley's Confederate forces neared Santa Fe, Judge Ellison, along with the Territorial government, fled for safety to Fort Union. It is not known whom Ellison left in charge of the mine.

On March 10, 1862, the Confederate Army entered Santa Fe. On March 24 a Confederate unit led by Sergeant Alfred B. Peticolas passed by the mine works at Dolores. "Spent ½ an hour in the mill very pleasantly and hear that the yield here is from $100 to $300 per ton of quartz*, and that the gold is worth 18 $ per oz. The quartz is crushed by huge beams that work up and down. It is a steam mill** and the machinery must have cost a good deal." [2] The mill was apparently functional, but it was not operating at the time Peticolas' unit was there. Sergeant Peticolas sketched the stamp mill building.

Gold mill - at Real de Dolores

Within a month all the Confederates were in full retreat from New Mexico.

---

* Equivalent to an incredibly high 5.5 to 16.5 ounces per ton.
** This particular steam engine probably arrived in 1859.

With Ellison absent, workmen were left either unsupervised or with unknown supervision. The amount of gold produced during the Civil War and the disposal of it are unknown, but there are several indications that some mining continued throughout the war years.

Eighteen sixty-three saw two University of Missouri classmates (Class of '60), who were to play significant roles in the story of New Mexico, on opposite sides in the Civil War. Twenty-two-year-old Captain Stephen B. Elkins, U.S.A., of the Kansas Militia served in the Union Army, and twenty-two-year-old Lieutenant Thomas B. Catron, C.S.A., was a gunnery officer assigned to Vicksburg. Catron's military career was interrupted that summer as he and his fellow Confederates at Vicksburg were besieged and then overrun and captured by an up and coming Union General, Ulysses S. Grant.

Soon after visiting Dolores with acting governor Arny, John Greiner reported to the N.M.M.C. in a letter dated February 7, 1863. "Coal of the very first quality and inexhaustible in quantity crops out of the bank three to four miles from the mill, where it has been worked in running the engine and in the shops of the blacksmith and machinist." [27]

Seven months later R. C. McCormick, Secretary of the Territory of Arizona, wrote another letter about the Ortiz mine to Colonel Puleston, soon to be the president of the N.M.M.C.; "There is already a fine steam engine and good machinery at the mines." [27][R. C. McCormick, Santa Fe, to Col. Puleston, Washington D.C., November 24, 1863]

- 82 -

In the same 1864 N.M.M.C. report is a passage that appears to indicate the company was trying to acquire yet another steam engine. "Considerable progress has been made in procuring machinery (including a fine steam-engine of forty-horse power),..." Moses Kelley, Secretary (N.M.M.C.). [27] Elsewhere in the report Kelly gives this characterization of the mines:

> "Only a small part of the 'Gold Region' has yet been dug, and experience has shown that the dust is about as likely to be found in one part of it as another... All the best diggings in the immediate vicinity of water however, seem pretty well excavated; in some places the hills and valleys are literally cut up like a honeycomb." [27]

In late 1864 geologists Professor Richard E. Owen and E. T. Cox, both associated with Indiana State University, were hired by Judge John S. Watts, one of the stockholders in the N.M.M.C., and others, to promote their mining properties. "Report on the Mines of New Mexico", a very upbeat report on the potential of the Ortiz mine and some other properties, was serialized in the November 23 and December 3, 1864, *Santa Fe Weekly Gazette*, and widely redistributed beginning in 1865. As Townley puts it, "The optimistic conclusions of their report were used by the company to substantiate the claims put forth in puffery published for eastern investors." [62]

In 1865 the principal stockholders in the N.M.M.C. were approached by George M. Willing, who owned a share in a placer claim near San Pedro, with a proposal to bring water from the Pecos River to the placers through ditches and pipelines. Willing suggested that if the placers could be hydraulically worked over $350 million in gold could be recovered. The cost of the project was estimated at $800,000. [62]

The proposal was argued at length in the newspapers and in the Legislature, but in the end the promoters were unable to secure the necessary funding. In 1867 a subsidiary of the N.M.M.C., the Pecos and Placer Mining and Ditch Company, was formed to pursue the Pecos plan through the private sector. Some money was raised, a few contracts were negotiated, some rights of way and parcels of land purchased, and even a "first shovel" ceremony was staged, but the grandiose project was much beyond the capacities and resources of the times, and was abandoned in 1868. However, more than once in the coming years the Pecos ditch proposal would rise again from its apparent grave.

The Civil War ended in June, 1865, and in August Michael Steck became the manager of the resurgent N.M.M.C.

Dr. Michael Steck arrived in New Mexico in early 1852 with Indian Agent-designate John Greiner, later replacing him in that office. Effective as territorial Indian Agent, Steck was ardently pro-Union. He disagreed with Civil War Indian policy, and resigned (or was removed) when General James H. Carleton settled the Navajos on the Bosque Redondo reservation.[26] On March 18, 1865, Michael Steck was replaced as Superintendent of Indian Affairs for the Territory of New Mexico by Felipe S. Delgado (one of the sons of Manuel Delgado, above). On June 1, 1865 Michael Steck, John Greiner, and Daniel Wright as partners filed two claims each for "a vein or deposit of metal" near Dolores,[52] [Book A, pp.43 & 45] the first of many claims the trio would develop.

The inflow of capital from assessments and the sale of new N.M.M.C. stock allowed Dr. Steck to go on a building binge.

Steck wrote from Kansas City on October 1st of 1865 to the company president, Dr. Thomas L. Kidwell of Washington D.C., that the 5-stamp ore-crushing mill and complete sawmill that he had purchased at St. Louis had been shipped by riverboat and were in his possession at Kansas City. Steck further informed Kidwell that he had arranged with an old experienced freighter named Charles G. Parker to deliver everything by wagon from Kansas City directly to the Ortiz mines in New Mexico. [56]

In late 1865 Parker transported nearly 13 tons of goods to the N.M.M.C. and was paid $2,055.20 for his services. As an indicator of the impact the coming railroad would have on the availability and cost of goods in New Mexico, it should be noted that Steck purchased all that machinery, some additional hardware, and a quantity of groceries for less than half as much as it cost to ship it all to Dolores. [56]

Steck says, "I have purchased... a five stamp mill [and] complete saw mill to attach to the company engine." [56] By 1866 cut dimensional lumber from the N.M.M.C mill was being sold in Santa Fe.

> As this history of the Ortiz Mountains is laden with so many firsts it is worth noting that the steam-powered sawmill at Dolores was only the SECOND steam-powered sawmill in New Mexico.

In addition to the new saw mill and stamp mill, Steck enlarged the stopes* of the Ortiz mine and extended the depth of the main shaft to 140 feet**, where he began to be hampered by groundwater. This rapid expansion also resulted in the accumulation of a large stockpile of uncrushed ore. This, combined with recently identified quantities of rich lode still in the mine, and flush with income from the flurry of gold production, in December of 1866 Steck decided to go

---

* A stope is an underground cavity created by the excavation of a block of ore.
** Miller's mid-1850s depth of the water table was given as 165 feet, as was Anderson's in 1870, and both of these probably refer to the Santa Rosalia shaft. The 140-foot figure is probably in reference to the Santo Niño - Tunia shaft.

again to St. Louis.

> "Dr. Steck of the Placer Mining Company of New Mexico arrived last Friday with a considerable amount of gold dust. He left an order for a 10-stamp mill. It is said that the quartz of Placer Mountain, about thirty miles from Santa Fe, turns out some $300 per cord. With a small 5-stamp mill, Dr. Steck extracted 200 ounces in the space of two months. These mines have been worked, at times, for some 150 years*. The present association is the result of efforts commenced five or six years ago, to establish a company for the reopening of the old works. Other lodes have been discovered in a westerly direction from this point, which give evidence of richness." [St. Louis Democrat, January 11, 1867]

The ten new stamps gave N.M.M.C. at least fifteen stamps, and they were all operational by August of 1867. This, of course, begs the question: what happened to the earlier Leitensdorfer-Rencher-Ellison stamps, which were mostly or entirely iron-capped logs with stone anvils? These may have been replaced by Steck's new all-metal stamps, as Townley suggests was the case. [62]

Steam powered stamps were the most efficient and productive method of pulverizing lode ores, and notwithstanding their expense, they were in great demand. General James H. Carleton, writing on January 13, 1866, mentions the old engine at the assemblage of 19 buildings at Real del Tuerto called the Ramirez Hacienda: "I visited the arastras, which were at work; saw the steam engine which is put up at the Hacienda, ..." [Letter from General James H. Carleton to Lt. Colonel A. B. Carey, January 13, 1866, pp 19-20, *Compleation of Facts, San Pedro & Canyon del Agua Grants*, Washington D.C., 1867]

But another letter describes this steam engine in such a way as to make it clear it was quite old and not of much use. Where do old steam engines come from? One can only speculate that this engine might have had an earlier life at the Dolores mill. [42]

---

* There is no known evidence to support this figure.

It was given to the press that by midsummer 1867 there were over 800 tons of $75 to $100 (per ton) ore stockpiled at the Dolores mill and awaiting processing, and the N.M.M.C. average cleanup during 1867 was $1800 per week. [53][SFWNM, June 8, 1867]

Around this time Steck also began the process of expelling the "trespass" miners who had been working within the boundaries of the Ortiz Mining Grant.

On November 11, 1865, Daniel Wright, acting as agent for John Greiner and Michael Steck, registered a 1500-foot long "anthracit" coal claim which he located about five miles northwest of Dolores. The coal bed was described as from 5 feet 8 inches to 5 feet 10 inches thick, in a "cañon or ravine which exhibit on its eastern wall columnar porphyry of fifty feet in height... and which porphyry again appears on the southern side of the hill..."* There was also "a ravine in which is the spring of water known as the 'ojito de carbon Piedra'** – a distance of about five hundred yards more or less from the opening of said bed of coal." The coal bed "is said to have been worked by a miner named Geronimo A_ at los Cerrillos*** many years since but the same has been abandoned by him and has not been legally denounced for more than ten years, although quantities of coal have been hauled therefrom by several persons in late years." This claim registration was signed by Daniel Wright and Theodore S. Greiner (a Notary Public and probable brother of John), but was

---

* This is probably a description of the ravine one-half mile south of modern Madrid.
** Little Coal spring.
*** A reference to the Alamo Creek area east of La Cienega, the location of Alfonso Rael de Aguilar's 1695 camp. It would be another fifteen years before the mining and railway town of Cerrillos was established seven miles to the south, at the confluence of San Marcos Arroyo and the Galisteo River.

specifically for the benefit of John Greiner and Michael Steck. [52][Book A #15405 p.69]

> This is in the same general area as the coal source utilized in 1860 to fuel the N.M.M.C. steam engine, and is also the future location of the town of Madrid. This coal claim was an attempt by Steck to secure for the company a reliable and protected supply of fuel. In this era the cost of coal fuel was half that of wood fuel. Even the Dolores blacksmith used coal rather than wood or charcoal. [62]

⁂

Late 1867 saw the arrival at Dolores of several wagons containing over nine tons of materials destined for a new 1.5-mile-long narrow-guage railroad. Once again C. G. Parker carried the goods, but this time from the railhead at Ellsworth, Kansas, now 200 miles nearer to Dolores than Kansas City, whence he had come two years earlier. Along with the half-ton of black powder and fuse and eight "pair axles wheels" (suggesting that the Dolores railroad was to operate with four cars), Parker's freight wagons carried a new steam boiler weighing all of 4300 pounds. [56]

The N.M.M.C. Report for 1868 gives more information. "In October last, 1867, a new stamp mill, of the James and Condict patent, in which the power is economized and the steam used to give force to the stamp, was purchased and sent out to the mines, costing the Company at the mines about $5500. The Superintendent*, for reason not fully disclosed, omitted all action towards the erection and running of this new mill until June, 1868, and although late advice informs us that it is now running, yet no sufficient test of its capacity has been made, ... Fred W. Jones, Sec. &

---

* Dr. Steck, who had also purchased a steam engine in 1866, at the time this stockholder's report was published had just retired from the company.

Treasurer (N.M.M.C.), September 30, 1868." [N.M.M.C. Report, 1868, p. 3]

The Dolores railroad, designed by Captain N. S. Davis, carried ore one-and-a-half miles from the Ortiz mine down the hill to the stamp mill next to Oso Springs. Until this mine car railroad began operating, most likely sometime early in 1868, the ore had to be carried by mules from the mine in small quantities down the steep trail to the processing area. This was expensive, and a bottleneck to production. With mules 20 tons of ore could be delivered to the mill. Steck's goal for the railroad was to deliver 100 tons a day. [62]

This Captain N. S. Davis is a cryptic character; possibly the same person as the contemporaneous Nathan S. Davis of Houston, Texas. He clearly had training or experience as a civil engineer. His name survives in New Mexico as Capt. Davis Mountain, an eastern outlier of the Ortiz Mountains, and in the name of the USGS Quadrangle map that covers much of the eastern Ortiz area.

After constructing the Ortiz railroad, Capt. Davis went to work in 1868 for the Moreno Water & Mining Company of Elizabeth-town, N.M., where he built the Big Ditch, an effort to channel water from the Red River to Elizabethtown for placering. The Big Ditch was completed on July 9, 1869, but had insufficient grade to deliver the amount of water required, and was not greatly successful. It was defunct by 1900. [9] Capt. Davis was also responsible for the rail line from Lordsburg, New Mexico, to Clifton, Arizona in the 1870s.

Around 1880 the N.M.M.C. revived the plan to deliver water from the Pecos River to the Ortiz Mine for hydraulic mining, and brought in Capt. Davis to lead the engineering effort. Schemes to bring water to the Ortiz had been an ongoing topic since the Civil War, but this time the proposal had the engineering skill of Capt. Davis and the backing of one of New Mexico's most important politicians, Tom Catron. In spite of these two big guns this Pecos aquaduct, too, foundered for lack of public interest and invest

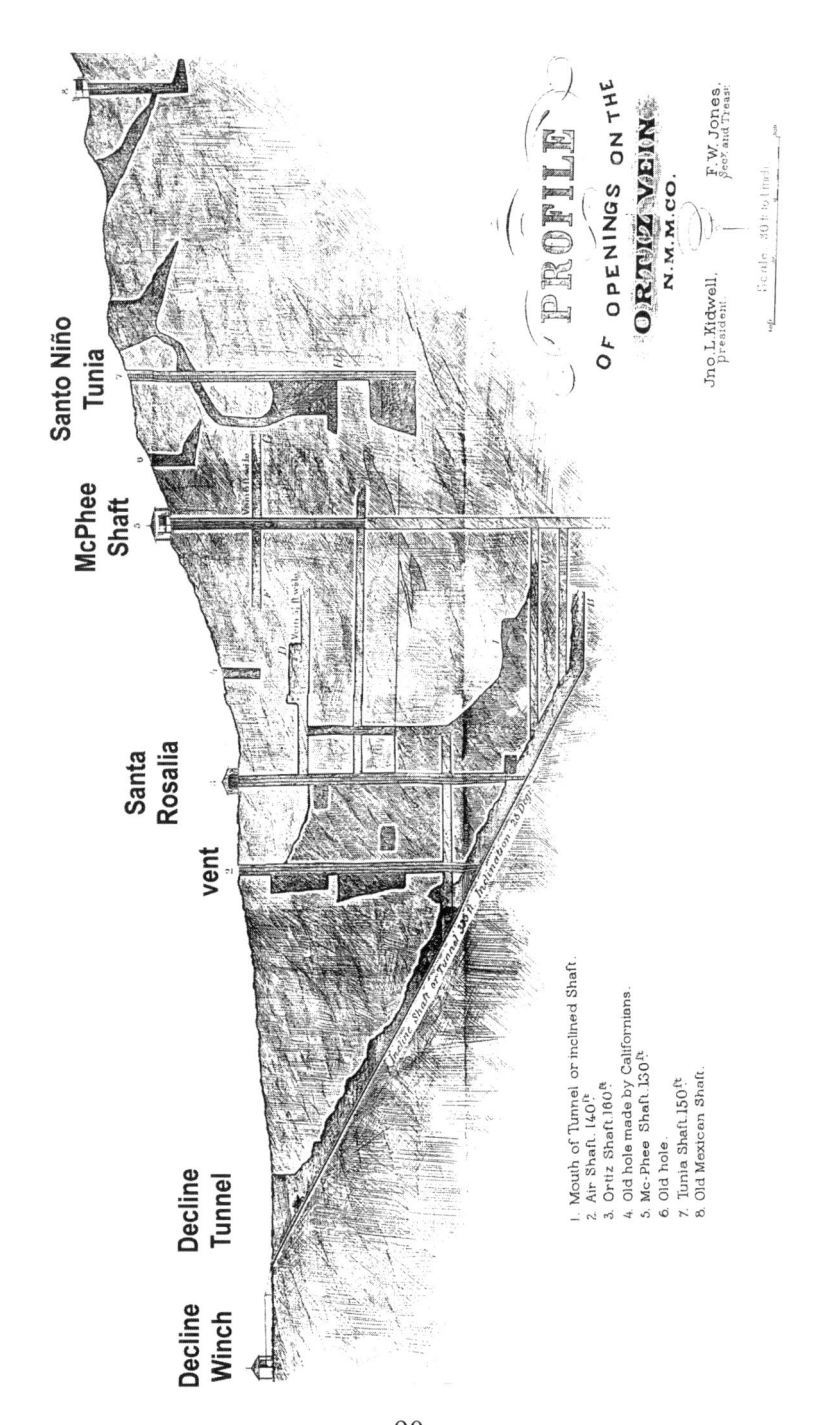

PROFILE
OF OPENINGS ON THE
ORTIZ VEIN
N.M.M.CO.

Jno. L. Kidwell,
President.

F. W. Jones,
Sec'y and Treas'r

Scale 50 ft to Inch

Decline Winch
Decline Tunnel
vent
Santa Rosalia
McPhee Shaft
Santo Niño Tunia

1. Mouth of Tunnel or Inclined Shaft.
2. Air Shaft. 140 ft
3. Ortiz Shaft. 160 ft
4. Old hole made by Californians.
5. Mc-Phee Shaft. 130 ft
6. Old hole.
7. Tunia Shaft. 150 ft
8. Old Mexican Shaft.

Left: The official N.M.M.C. cut-away profile of the Ortiz mine complex circa 1868 (captions added). Northeast is right, southwest is left. Four winches are represented, all probably hand powered, though this is unclear in the case of the decline winch (see detail below). The absence of a winch atop the Tunia shaft implies it was not being worked at this time.

This document is the only instance of this name (McPhee) for the intermediate shaft. That shaft was filled and covered with a carpet of rocks in 2002 by the New Mexico M.M.D. Abandoned Mine Land Bureau.

Compare this diagram with the Old Ortiz Mine cross section below.

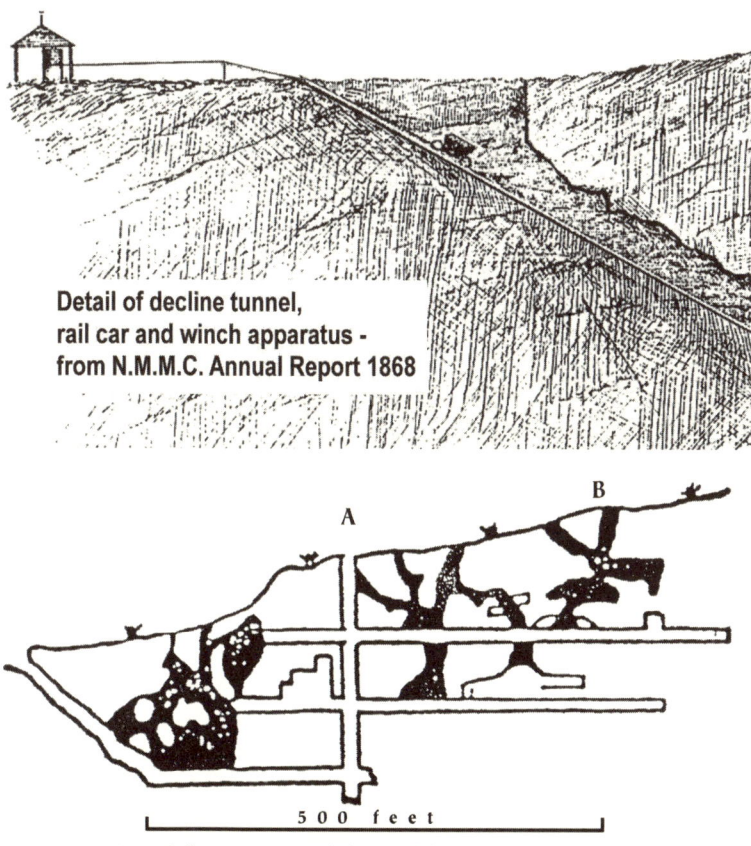

Detail of decline tunnel, rail car and winch apparatus - from N.M.M.C. Annual Report 1868

Cross section of the Ortiz mine (A). Old Santo Niño Tunia shaft is (B). Shaded areas are stopes excavated during Mexican era, prior to 1850.

ment, and the inability to obtain government approval. Another project that same year, one aimed at discovering "Artesian wells" on the Ortiz Mining Grant, also failed.[61]

A decline* was dug on the south side of the Ortiz mine and the tram cars were rolled through it into the mine where they were loaded with ore. The loaded cars were then winched by cable up the decline to the surface, and powered by gravity and controlled by brakes, were rolled down the long, steep hill to the mill. Empty cars were pulled by mules back up the hill to the mine. Initially, the rails of the Ortiz railroad were made of hardwood set on piñon crossties, except for the few curved portions where the rails were of iron.

"There were problems with the Ortiz railroad. The broken wheel holders along the track show that. However, the immense effort that went into the project – the walls of stone to maintain the track at a constant grade – is impressive."[42] The full story of the railroad came out in the N.M.M.C. 1868 Annual Report.

"A railroad or tramway of wooden rails has been constructed, which leads from the mines to the old mill at the village of Real de Dolores, and from thence has been continued to the new mill at the lower village, Las Norias, the total length of which is about two miles. Like many other improvements of this kind, the cost of this road has very far exceeded the cost estimated before its inception, and it is quite probable that it would have remained unconstricted had the Board been fully advised of the sum it would cost.

"The Superintendent [Dr. Steck] gave as his estimate of the cost of this improvement the sum of $3340, which he afterwards increased to the sum of $7542, upon the report of a practical civil engineer [Capt. Davis], who surveyed the line of the road and made full and specific estimates for the excavations, fillings, and

---

* A tunnel leading down at an angle from the surface.

The entrance to the Old Ortiz decline, 2003. (Historical figure included for scale.)
Photo courtesy of Charles Strom

the entire grading, and also the bridges, cross-ties, rails, keys, &c., and upon this information the construction of the road was ordered. The actual cost, however, approximated $17,000; considerably more than twice the estimated cost as given by an apparently intelligent and practical engineer. This discrepancy is only partially accounted for by the unexpectedly large amount of blasting out and other unusual expenses in preparing the road-bed, through an exceedingly rocky and otherwise rough location; and the true solution is found in a lack of good management, which manifested itself in an entire cessation of efforts at gold production during the progress of the construction of the railroad, which monopolized the entire time and labor of all the employees of the Company, and permitted the gold-producing machinery to remain entirely inactive.

"The durability of wooden rails was also inaccurately stated, when the construction of the railroad was being urged upon the Board. It was said that except at the curves, where they would require the additional strength of an iron rail, the wooden rails would serve for several years, the attrition being slight, and sufficient rails of steel for these curves were sent out. It is now found that the entire track must be ironed, the wooden rails being

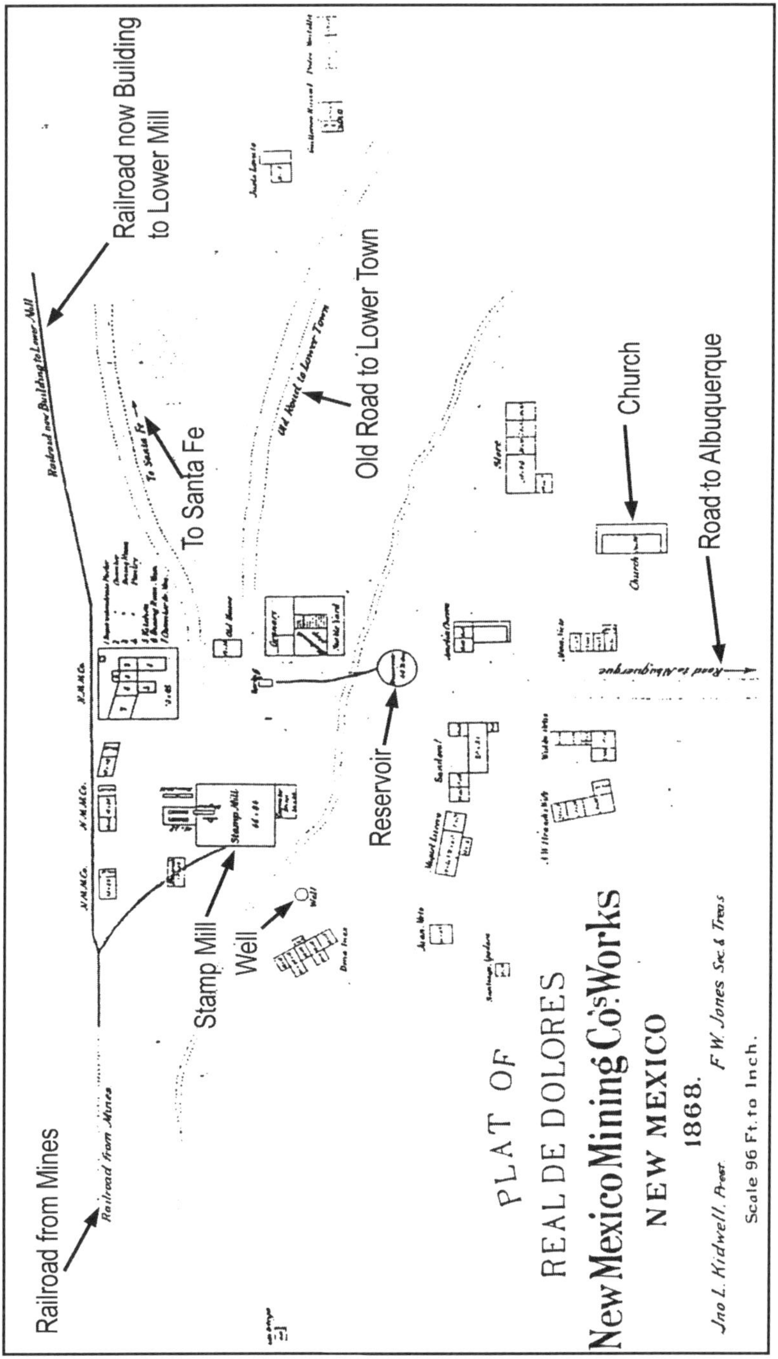
Railroad from Mines
Railroad now Building to Lower Mill
To Santa Fe
Old Road to Lower Town
Church
Road to Albuquerque
Reservoir
Stamp Mill
Well
PLAT OF
REAL DE DOLORES
New Mexico Mining Co's Works
NEW MEXICO
1868.
Jno L. Kidwell, Prest.
F.W. Jones Sec. & Treas.
Scale 96 Ft. to Inch.

The land contours on this 1876 map are inexact, but it shows the Ortiz – Dolores rail line, which was by this time defunct. Note the road to Santa Fe, which forded Galisteo Creek not far from the modern SR-14 – CR-55A junction, and which touches at San Marcos spring. The road going south from Real de Dolores to Real de San Francisco (Golden) passes between Cunningham Hill and Capt. Davis Mountain. The towns of Cerrillos and Madrid do not yet exist. Four years after this map was composed the A.T.& S.F. would lay its tracks along Galisteo Creek.
Wheeler Survey Map 77B, originally issued May 7, 1877

entirely inadequate for the work. This necessity so increased the expense attendant on the railroad, that when it is fully complete, its entire cost will approximate $25,000. The iron rails with the necessary accompaniment of spikes, &c., have been purchased and sent out to the mines, and it is fully expected that the entire line of road will be completed this Autumn, or by the 1st day of December A.D. 1868.

> "While the cost of the railroad has been great, it would be injust to omit referring to its marked utility and value to us, and it is not unreasonable to state that the economy in transportation will more than suffice to repay the cost of the railroad in a very few years. Heretofore the transportation of quartz has been at an expense of about $3 per ton, and it will now cost not over 25 cts. The railroad also serves for the transportation of wood, and is in every way a most desirable adjunct to the Company's operations." [1868 N.M.M.C. annual report to the stockholders]

During 1868 approximately 15,000 feet of 3/8-inch by 1 1/4-inch machine-rolled iron strip, with lathe-drilled countersunk spike holes [42] was delivered to Dolores. These iron strips were laid atop the wooden rails as armor, and at the end of the year the railroad was finally operational.

An 1868 map of the area shows the rails extending to a "Lower Mill" in the area known as Las Norias. Despite the statement in the annual report, there is no good evidence the railroad extension north to the Las Norias mill was ever realized.

The Ortiz railroad was operational for at least two years, but not more than four. The burden of the unexpected expense of 'ironing' the wooden rails and the rapid depletion of the free milling ore at the Ortiz mine were major factors in its short life.

Capt. Davis' Ortiz gravity and mule railroad was the first railroad built in New Mexico and the first railroad in all of the Rocky Mountains.

In late 1868, with N.M.M.C. profits apparently the largest ever, and stock at all time highs, Dr. Steck resigned from the company, retiring to his home in Pennsylvania a wealthy man. In fact, Steck's expenditures on mine and mill development and for the railroad had outstripped revenues, but this was not immediately obvious. [40]

(Bell 1870)

In 1867 and 1868 William A. Bell, as part of a survey of possible railroad routes in the west, visited Dolores and witnessed Steck's new stamp mill in operation.

> "The ore after being broken into small pieces, is thrown into the long troughs into which the three sets of crushers – five to a set – descend. The crushers are given a rotary motion as they fall, so that they grind and crush the ore at the same time. When the ore has been reduced to a muddy slime by the mixture with water under the crushing process, it percolates through sieves into the shallow copper trays which are seen in front of the picture. These trays are coated with quicksilver, which sucks up the gold, swells to thrice its size, and forms an amalgam containing about two-thirds gold. This is scraped off, tied up in a piece of rag, and

placed in a crucible for reduction. A dull red heat is necessary to drive off the quicksilver and leave the gold behind it in a state of purity. The men in the foreground are in the act of cleaning the copper trays with cyanide of potassium preparatory to recoating them with a thin film of quicksilver." [6]

<hr>

Col. A. L. Anderson, formerly U.S. Army Corps of Engineers, after being familiarized with the operations by Steck, replaced Steck as N.M.M.C. manager. Col. Anderson, who continued Steck's spending spree and inherited Steck's debts, did not inherit his good luck.

Anderson expanded upon Steck's large crew, eventually employing 40 miners and 16 support personnel. Like Steck, Anderson actively discouraged private prospecting and mining on the Ortiz Grant. He increased ore production by opening up the Brehm lode, a low-grade free milling gold vein near the Ortiz mine. The additional ore seriously exceeded the capacity of the Dolores mill, and quantities began to be stockpiled.

In January 1869 Anderson traveled to the east to acquire 25 additional stamps for the then 15-stamp mill. Upon his return, April 1869, construction was begun on a new building to house the combined forty stamps. The construction project diverted workers from mining and immediately affected production, but it was hoped that the increased capacity, expected to be 160 tons per day, would make up for the lost revenue. [62]

> Each of the new 650-pound stamps dropped at a rate of 75 times a minute.

But there were some problems with the installation of the new mill. And Anderson had not felt it necessary to dig exploratory drifts to determine the actual extent of the remaining free milling ore body, so just when his capacity to process peaked his supply of ore petered out. As well, by 1870 the free milling lode had been mined down to the 165-foot groundwater level [61] at which point the presence of massive sulphides required more complex and expensive processing, considerably beyond the capabilities of the N.M.M.C.

> Lode ore veins in the Ortiz are composed of porous quartz containing pyrites (iron-sulfur or iron-arsenic compounds) and tiny flakes or threads of free gold. The higher portions of the lode veins, those above the geological water table, had been exposed to air (oxygen) for millions of years and the pyrites were converted to oxides and chlorides. Below the water table they had not been converted and remained sulfides. [42]
>
> Oxidation of gold-bearing sulfide ores helps free the gold and facilitates its erosion and sedimentary reconcentration. [24]

By April of 1869 the company's financial situation was precarious. [61] David P. Staley suggests it was Anderson's stockpiling of ores, his 1869 purchases, and his large payroll, and not Steck's management, that was the cause of the difficulties to come. [64] Whatever the cause, the N.M.M.C.'s ever-deepening distress led directly to the replacement of Col. Anderson, and ultimately to Elkins and Chaffee gaining control of the company.

In 1870 Col. Anderson was replaced as manager by W. C. Rencher, the second son of former Governor Abraham Rencher, and a major stockholder in the N.M.M.C. in his own right. Later Rencher would become the editor of the *Santa Fe Democrat* newspaper. Once in control of the Ortiz mine Rencher focused on removing the remaining free milling ore from the pillars and the sides of the old stopes. In June of 1870 all 40 stamps were reported operating at the Dolores mill, though Raymond [48] [1874] reported there were 20 stamps operating and 20 more standing by. The apparent bustle was a false prosperity. The free milling supply ran out and the mine was on standby status. [62] In 1871 the Ortiz Mine was closed.

In 1873, two years after the Ortiz mine had closed, the Ortiz-Dolores railroad was reported as "somewhat out of repair". [49]

In the following years the mine was leased several times to various parties, but it never regained the stature or prosperity it appeared to have in the later 1860s.

The town of Dolores got its first U.S. Post Office in March of 1869, with William H. Roberts as postmaster, but it was shut down the next year, and the mine the following year. When the N.M.M.C. reopened the Grant to private miners in 1887 and the population spiked, the Dolores Post Office reopened with postmaster Alfred Wolf. In 1890 it was closed for the second time. The third and last incarnation of the Dolores Post Office lasted from 1897 to 1901 with Hiram Haines as postmaster. The 1901 shutdown was permanent. [47] The inhabitants of ghost towns don't depend much upon post offices.

Dolores was first identified as a specific locality in the census of 1870. Whereas in the boom times of the 1830s the whole of the Ortiz Mountains had a regular winter population of several thousand, and the 1846-47 estimated population was 200, the 1870 Census found 183 people living in Dolores in 63 dwellings and 11 other structures. They were 92% with Hispanic surname and 98% of those New Mexico born. There were 1.3 males over 15 years of age for each female over 15, and 43 children (15 and under). Nearly a quarter of the population of Dolores were children!

In the mid 70s, after the closing of the Ortiz mine, the population was estimated at 150. By 1879, with the Grant again open to private miners, it was back up to 200.

The Census of 1880 found 144 people in 37 dwellings, over 98% Hispanic and all of those born in New Mexico. The adult ratio was the same as ten years earlier – 1.3 to 1 – and there were 45 children – over 30%. Only seventeen names from the 1870 Census are also on the 1880 Census. Of note, no one on the 1880 Census gave his occupation as "miner", possibly because the N.M.M.C. had prohibited private mining within the Ortiz Grant. By 1893 the population of Dolores was estimated at 100.

"In all the little stores here gold dust passes current, and each can show you a bottle heavy with the beautiful stuff. It isn't quite as handy as greenbacks, but it looks a heap better."[35] [Charles Lummis, reporting from Golden in December, 1884]

A derelict 10-stamp mill in the Ortiz Mountains.
Lucien A. File Collection #1971-006, courtesy New Mexico State Archives Image #55571

Stephen B. Elkins

Through a combination of overspending and poor mining results the New Mexico Mining Company found itself in trouble and in desperate need of new capital.

In 1878 control of the N.M.M.C. was acquired by two wealthy and powerful men: Steven B. Elkins, the former U.S. Attorney General for the Territory of New Mexico (1869-70) and the Territorial Delegate to Congress (1873-77), and Jerome B. Chaffee of Leadville and Denver, Colorado, who had made his fortune at the Leadville mines. Neither Chaffee nor Elkins (since 1873) were residents of New Mexico.

There had been other attempts to gain control of the shaky company with the large land holdings, but Chaffee and Elkins succeeded. For the next thirty years until the Ortiz Grant was leased to the Hoyts in 1900, Elkins remained its largest stockholder and maintained control of the company.

From 1864 to 1888 the swath of Stephen Benton Elkins streaked across the Territory of New Mexico. He had few rivals and no peers, enormous power and growing wealth, and many enemies. His star protogé and one-time classmate, Thomas Benton Catron, who in 1866 accompanied Elkins from Missouri to New Mexico, learning Spanish along the way, eventually filled his shoes. In time Tom Catron would inherit the power in New Mexico, and the wealth and the enemies that went with it.

Elkins was born in 1841 in Ohio, grew up in Missouri, attended the University of Missouri at Columbia, and served as a Captain in the Kansas Militia. In late 1863 he moved to Mesilla, New Mexico, where he was admitted to the bar, and from 1864 to 1865 served in the Territorial House of Representatives. From 1866 (after that trip to Missouri, where he also married Sarah Jacobs) to 1867 he was Territorial District Attorney, then, in

1869, U.S. Attorney General for the Territory.

Eighteen sixty nine is generally regarded as the year a powerful group of lawyer-politician-businessmen in Santa Fe, led by Stephen B. Elkins, Thomas B. Catron, and Stephen W. Dorsey, became a force to be reckoned with. The year 1869 saw the rise of the (predominantly but by no means entirely Republican) Santa Fe Ring.

Senator Stephen B. Elkins, 1895
Photo courtesy NM MMD

As an example of the excesses of this group, in 1869, after Interior Secretary J.D. Cox had determined the Maxwell Land Grant contained about 96,000 acres, Elkins, Catron, Dorsey, Frank Springer and others arranged a survey that measured it as 1,714,764 acres. After massaging the grant to 18 times larger than originally determined, Elkins attempted to have his survey paid for out of public funds!

From March 1873 to March 1877 Elkins served as the New Mexico Territorial Delegate (R) to Congress, and from that time he was no longer resident in New Mexico, though he was a frequent visitor.

In 1878, the same year Elkins and Chaffee acquired control of the Ortiz Grant, Elkins, Catron and others hired a Colorado miner named Robert Hart to develop their Cerrillos Hills properties. Hart's efforts were unexpectedly successful, and set off the great Cerrillos mining boom of 1879-1884.

Charles Lummis, a staunch Republican himself and soon to be editor of the Los Angeles Times, reporting from New Placer in 1884, says, "Steve Elkins is the boss thief of the lot, and he is a choice one. He is universally detested and feared throughout all New Mexico, and his life wouldn't be worth much if he were to venture into this part of the country."[35]

In 1888 Elkins became a resident of West Virginia, where he was elected U.S. Senator, according to the practice of the time, by the state legislature. He held that office continuously – except for 1891 to 1893 when he was Secretary of War – until his death in 1911. But in absentia he continued to wheel and deal in New Mexico. In 1891 he sold the Madrid properties (the Cerrillos Coal & Iron Company, which he did not fully own) to the Atchison, Topeka & Santa Fe Rail Road. In September of 1899, on behalf of the N.M.M.C., he sold to the Hoyt brothers of New York a 99-year lease on the Ortiz Grant.

Thomas Benton Catron was born October 6, 1840 near Lexington, Missouri. He graduated from the University of Missouri at Columbia, Class of 1860. In the Civil War he saw action as a Lieutenant, C.S.A., in Lowe's Missouri Battery in the siege of Vicksburg, where he was taken prisoner. Later freed by a prisoner exchange, Catron served the South (and survived) until the end. In 1866 he

Senator Thomas B. Catron
Photo credit U.S. Senate Historical Office

was convinced by his former classmate, Stephen B. Elkins, to leave Missouri for the Territory of New Mexico – probably not hard to do, as there were restrictions placed upon the political or legal career options for former Confederates in the United States that did not apply in the Territories – where in 1867 at Las Cruces, he changed his party afiliation from Democrat to Republican, and set up a commercial law practice.

He was the District Attorney for New Mexico's Third District until 1868. In 1869 he was appointed Territorial Attorney General. In 1872 he resigned to take the position of the United States Attorney, which he held until 1878.

As a rule Tom Catron occupied his mentor and friend Elkins' political offices as Elkins moved on to higher ones. Like Elkins, Catron became an important part the Santa Fe Ring, and participated in the Maxwell land manipulation. In 1872 he was one of the founding members – it is no surprise that Elkins was another – of the Consolidated Land, Cattle Raising & Wool Growing Company, the first cattle company incorporated in New Mexico, and for the next nine years the only such company in the state.

Interestingly, on October 5, 1875 Tom Catron seems to have personally staked out a 20-acre placer claim in the New Placer [52] [Book A, p.302], and apparently, whatever he learned from this experience led him never to repeat it.

Catron was the attorney in fact for Stephen Elkins while Elkins was in and out of New Mexico as Territorial Delegate, and after Elkins moved permanently to New York City and West Virginia. Catron was also, in part, responsible for the Cerrillos mining boom, he managed the sale of much of the Cerrillos townsite on Elkins' behalf, and he probably chose the name for the camp along the approaching railroad: "Cerrillos Station", without the "Los".

From 1884, off and on until statehood in 1912, Catron served on the New Mexico Territorial Council. (He lost in the elections of 1892 and 1896.) Though Tom Catron didn't win all his battles, he was always there and always in the contest, and he won more than his share. Along the way he managed to amass enormous landholdings in New Mexico, some of which were widely believed to have been acquired through misrepresentation and malfeasance.

Former New Mexico Governor Lew Wallace (in office 1878-81), also a Republican, gave a revealing characterization of Tom Catron in a letter he wrote in 1897 to a friend in Santa Fe who was about to lose to Harry S. Clancy for the office of U.S. District Attorney. "It seems impossible to me that the President should make the mistake of appointing Mr. Clancy, who, although a very clever gentleman, must necessarily be a retainer of Mr. Catron. That Governor Oterro has submitted himself to the domination of Mr. Catron does not surprise me. One of the curious incidences pertaining to Mr. Catron is his astonishing influence over New Mexicans. I cannot recall one instance in which he did not absolutely submerge and control all persons who came in contact with him speaking the Spanish tongue."

Upon statehood in 1912 Tom Catron became the first Senator from New Mexico, and he served in that office for five years. He died on May 15, 1921.

Jerome Bunty Chaffee, a native of New York, in lucrative partnership with Stephen B. Elkins negotiated the sale of the Maxwell Land Grant to a Dutch-English syndicate. Chaffee further prospered from his investments in Leadville, Colorado, mines, served as Colorado's first territorial delegate to Congress (Republican), and at statehood in 1876 became one of its first U.S. senators.

Senator Jerome B. Chaffee
Photo credit U.S. Senate Historical Office

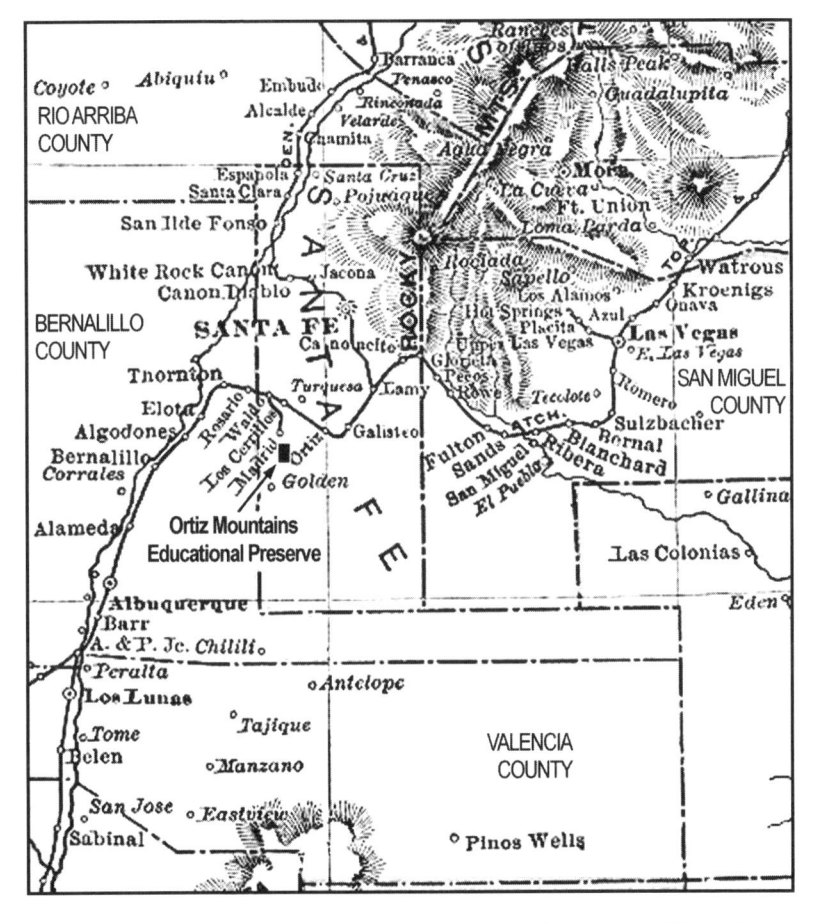

A portion of an 1895 railroad map of New Mexico and the location of the Ortiz Mountains Educational Preserve. The railroad towns of Ortiz, Waldo and Rosario would all give up the ghost in the twentieth century. Thornton is modern Domingo. Yet to come were Torrance, Sandoval and Los Alamos counties.

Early in 1880 the tracks of the Atchison, Topeka & Santa Fe Rail Road (really the New Mexico & Southern Pacific R. R., inasmuch as the Atchison, Topeka & Santa Fe line ended technically at its destination, Santa Fe) reached Cerrillos Station, and the world changed. Immediately, transportation became easy and cheap. Now bulk cargos such as coal and machinery and livestock could be shipped over long distances. And the railroad brought with it jobs. The railroad needed workers for the line, cut timber for ties, and water and coal for its steam engines. The railroad, however, was of little benefit to the Ortiz mine, which had just about exhausted the gold accessible by existing technology.

On the other hand the promotional possibilities for the New Mexico mines were enhanced because now Eastern dignitaries and politicians could more easily visit them. One of the most famous and first of these was former President Ulysses S. Grant, who on visiting Santa Fe in the summer of 1880, and upon being offered the office of president of the San Pedro & Cañon del Agua Mining Company, personally inspected the operations and camp at New Placer*. Though initially agreeable, Grant eventually declined that offer. [3, 42]

D. A. Millington, a reporter for the Kansas City Journal, having visited Cerrillos Station and Old and New Placers, filed the following dispatch on February 17, 1880.

> "...to Cerrillos station, on the Gallistes river. Here the track layers were in force, laying a switch on which to run a long train of freight cars, which was standing on the main track.** Here is being constructed a large smelter and reduction works by the Carpenter company.*** Here also are extensive coal mines. From thence we passed on south up a high mesa and long slope seven miles to Old Placers, which is an old Mexican town and around which are extensive placer gold diggings in the bars of streams and beneath the terminal moraine of an ancient glacier.**** Here, also, is a large forty stamp mill, large steam

---

* Until the twentieth century the main road from Cerrillos Station to New Placer passed through Dolores. See the 1868 Dolores Plat, page 94, for "Road to Albuquerque", and also the 1876 map on page 95.
** The New Mexico & Southern Pacific incarnation of the AT&SF railroad (see pages 106-07) was under construction. It had reached Galisteo Junction (Lamy) on February 9, 1880 and would be in Albuquerque by mid April.
*** H. H. Carpenter's New York & New Mexico Mining & Smelting Company plant was built east of where Mary's Bar and The Whatnot Shop are today.
**** Millington's geology is faulty here.

works for the reduction of the gold bearing quartz in the adjacent mountains. This mill has not been run of late for want of water. These mines are on a grant known as the Ortiz grant, ten miles square, and has been recently purchased by Elkins and others for $1,500,000, and the works are to be refitted and supplied with water by tubes from the head of the Pecos river, thirty-five miles off.*

"The placer mines were worked extensively by the Spaniards before 1680** and were evidently rich, but at present cannot be worked extensively for want of water. We passed on around and through the mountain gorges to the south and west ten miles to New Placers, where we found a Mexican town and put up for the night with a Yankee family in an adobe house which was bright and comfortable. We did not conclude that the placer mines were paying very well, but, scattered through the adjacent mountains, were many fissure mines now being prospected and opened, containing good prospects of gold and silver, some having a large percentage of lead, others of copper, and others of zinc."

In 1884 the N.M.M.C. sold to its major shareholders, Elkins and Chaffee – this was essentially Elkins and Chaffee selling to Elkins and Chaffee – the 15,026-acre Madrid tract. Gold mining might be nearly bust, but with the new railroad coal had a bright future. Elkins and Chaffee spun off the coal resources of the Ortiz Grant to the Cerrillos Coal and Iron Company (C.C. & I.C.), which was formed to develop the Madrid coal field. By this transaction the size of the Ortiz Grant was reduced to 57,267 acres.

For many years people had been mining coal from the Coal Bank beds, and one of the initial objectives of the C.C. & I.C. was to formalize this arrangement with the small operators. But the company's control of the coal mining fell apart in the late 1880s because of poor management. There was no one on the scene to collect

---

* A reference to the recurring effort to use Pecos water for hydraulic mining.
** No known evidence supports this date.

rent from miners, who quickly learned they did not have to sign a lease to mine coal in the Madrid Tract. [42]

Meanwhile, up in the mountains, the N.M.M.C. was frustrated by its inability to make the Ortiz gold mining operation profitable. In the late 1880s the N.M.M.C. began to open up the grant to leases by outside miners, making the policy official in 1887. Lode mines could be had on 99-year leases, and placer claims for a percentage of the takings.

By 1887 the cyanidation process for extracting gold from ores began to supplant mercury amalgamation. Also, other processes using electro-refining (the Moebius and Thum Balbach processes) were newly available. Both of these technologies were to have a profound effect on the quest for the gold of the Ortiz, but their greatest impact was yet far in the future.

On March 4, 1873, Elkins was elected Territorial Representative for New Mexico, and he established his residence in Washington, D.C. He was reelected in 1875, but did not stand again for the office in 1877. He moved to New York City, and then, in 1888, to advance his political career, to the state of West Virginia, where he was immediately elected U. S. Senator by the state legislature*.

With Elkins' political connections and growing power he was able to defend the interests of the N.M.M.C. with great success – no small achievement, as

---

* Until 1913 U.S. Senators were selected by the various state legislatures. In 1913 popular election of Senators was instituted.

there were numerous suits from stockholders and other claimants. Two of the lawsuits got as far as the Supreme Court.

A significant result of Senator Elkins' new position was manifest the following year, when, on October 2, 1889 – a full thirty-six years after John Greiner's original acquisition of some interest in the Santa Rosalia and Santo Niño claims, and twenty-eight years after the House of Representatives approved the Ortiz Mine Claim – the N.M.M.C. secured from the United States Congress the full and clear title (a quit-claim patent) to the Ortiz-Cano Ortiz Mining Grant.

But in this moment of victory the company was in dire straits; once again nearly bankrupt. The N.M.M.C. was unable to interest investors or to raise capital. Elkins was compelled to action.

In the early 1890s Senator Elkins' brother, Samuel H. Elkins, came to New Mexico to manage some of his brother's N.M.M.C. interests, which included the Sandia Mining Company's Cunningham deposit diggings. In 1893, employing 125 to 150 men, he intensively worked some rich, shallow, placer gold deposits on Cunningham Mesa, exhausting those deposits within one year.

In 1891 the Senator sent as his agent his long time friend, Richard C. Kerens, to New Mexico to assert Cerrillos Coal and Iron Company ownership over the Madrid Tract. Kerens began to evict the squatters. In a secret deal with the A.T.&S.F signed on on December 10, 1891 – the secrecy was essential because Elkins did not fully own the company at the time – Elkins and Kerens sold the entire C.C. & I.C. to the Atchison, Topeka & Santa Fe for $600,000 in bonds and some portion of a $400,000 cash payment. In early 1892

Elkins and Kerens formed the Cerrillos Coal Railroad Company (C.C.R.C.) as the holding company for the Madrid Tract. Virtually all of the C.C.R.C. stock went to the A.T.&S.F., while Elkins and Kerens took the company's bonds. The A.T.&S.F. so mismanaged the C.C.R.C. that barely ten years later it was reorganized out of existence.[42] It is not known if Elkins or Kerens ever realized any proceeds from the bonds, ostensibly worth $600,000.

Kerens removed the squatters at the coal mines by whatever means necessary (money, threats, dynamite)[42] and they were gone by the summer of 1892. In that year the 6.5-mile long standard-gauge railroad spur was built by the A.T.&S.F. from Waldo Station on the main line to the Madrid coal mines. In late 1892 "Madrid Siding" appears as a named locality, and the town of Madrid grew up around Keren's* house there.

For more than the next fifty years, and under the hegemony of a series of different landlords, Madrid** was fated to exist as a tightly regimented coal-mining company town.

Also in 1893, Congress repealed the Silver Purchasing Act of 1890, and this death blow to silver mining marked the beginning of a five-year long national economic collapse. The population of Real de Dolores in 1893 was reported to be 100.

---

* Richard C. Kerens, who financed the Madrid project with his own money, was an important figure in Republican circles, eventually becoming the U.S. Ambassador to Austro-Hungary (1910-1913). He died in St. Louis in 1916.

** Madrid's most famous native, Mary Wayne Marsh, was born in Madrid on November 9th, 1895. D.W. Griffith changed her name to Mae Marsh, and she starred in his classic silent films INTOLERANCE and THE BIRTH OF A NATION. Her last major movie role was in HOW GREEN WAS MY VALLEY, in 1941.

In the same year (1893) the inhabitants of Dolores asserted themselves with righteous confidence. It is not likely they were aware of the risk of their action, nor would they have believed an adverse outcome possible, but in the end what they did led to the final demise of Dolores.

Guadalupe Montoya, for himself and on behalf of the other inhabitants of Real de Dolores del Oro, filed suit in the United States Court of Private Land Claims for confirmation of four square leagues of property centered about the church at Dolores. The citizens of the town asserted that in 1830 Governor José Antonio Cháves had formed the town of Dolores under Mexican law, and as they and their ancestors had lived there for more than a lifetime, the land was rightfully theirs.

Looking east at the church *Nuestra Señora de los Dolores* in its cleaned-up glory. H. Milford suggests the pitched, sheet-metal roof may have been taken from an abandoned store in Dolores as an easier way to fix an old and leaking flat roof. The date of this photograph is unknown. It may be from before the turn of the century, as an assertion of community ownership in support of the pending land claim suit, or it may be after 1905 (see the photo on page 123).
Courtesy Museum of New Mexico Neg.#28496

Four years later (1897) Governor Otero, the first Hispanic governor of the Territory, denied the claim, saying that the Ortiz Mine Grant was a valid patent. Two years later the Supreme Court upheld the Governor's judgment. The people of Dolores, some of whom might have been able to trace family occupation back seventy years or more, had no claim to their town nor to any lands in it or near it. [7]

Whereas in the census of 1870 thirty-one Dolores respondents said they owned their houses, in 1900, with nearly the same population, only three indicated that they owned their houses. The statement by those three was an open yet futile denial of the recent Supreme Court decision.

Though it should have been evident to all that the time of free milling gold and small family placers in the Ortiz was gone – indeed, the settlement of Dolores was all but dead – the spirit of the miner persisted. Famously, the sole requirement of he who would be a miner has always been unflinching optimism in the face of all evidence to the contrary.

⁂

The following two upbeat items appeared in 1896 in area newspapers.

> "Commencing about four miles south of the flourishing town of Cerrillos, Santa Fe county, and extending south for twelve or more miles, in disconnected ranges of mountains and hills, with an average width of six miles, is one of the richest and most wonderful mineral regions in New Mexico. The geological formation, and the surface mineral indications of this entire section, are, without peradventure, unequaled in the great southwest. Within this section are situated the mining towns of San Pedro, Golden and Dolores." [W. M. Emmert in The Mines of New Mexico, 1896]

"The new dam below the Ortiz mining company's mill, at Dolores, was completed early this week, and the reservoir is now accumulating water. The mill will start up in the expectation of continuous work at once. Superintendent Strickland will ship another carload of ore early next week." [Cerrillos Rustler, cited in The Mines of New Mexico, 1896]

The Old Ortiz Mine works, 1905. The shed to the upper right appears to be a headframe over the McPhee shaft. The center structure is the power house – note the tall smoke stack for the steam engine. A portion of that smoke stack – a rivetted helical tube – may be seen there today. The ore was processed in the large building to the left, which may have also housed the stone-filled wheel pictured on page 49.
Photo by L.C. Graton, courtesy U.S.Geological Survey

In May of 1897 the N.M.M.C. was on the verge of foreclosure from bond holders, like the Hoyts, and creditors. It reorganized and leased its best properties, the Ortiz, Cunningham and Brehm lodes, to the Missouri-Kansas Syndicate, which tried to make a go of it. But in 1898 the Syndicate was forced to terminate the lease. Samuel H. Elkins (see page 111) was appointed by the Court as receiver of the N.M.M.C., and he supervised the subsequent sale of a 99-year lease to the Hoyts. [42]

The Cerrillos Coal Rail Road Company, until then a subsidiary of the A.T.&S.F., was dissolved in 1901 and reconstituted as part of the A.T.&S.F.

Around 1899 the number of sheep in New Mexico peaked at about 5 million, or nearly ten times the number today. There are still to be seen in the lower areas of the Ortiz Mountains several thirty- and fifty-yard long alignments of large stones, the remnants of the once numerous sheep pens.

Thomas Edison

In 1896 or 1897 N.M.M.C. hired an English mining engineer, Samuel G. Burn, to make a report on the minerals in the Ortiz Grant. Burn's 1897 report painted a very rosy picture, even an unrealistic picture, which indicated large placer fields of over 25 cents in gold per cubic yard.

About the time of Burn's survey Stephen B. Elkins and the other owners of the Ortiz grant had been talking to Thomas Edison about the possibility that his new and secret dry ore separation process would work in the Ortiz, but had come to the conclusion that it wasn't for them. So they took Burn's survey and talked the three Hoyt brothers (who had offices in the same building in New York City that Elkins did*) into taking a 99-year lease on the Ortiz property from N.M.M.C. for quite a lot of money. They suggested, with Burn's report as evidence, that the Hoyt brothers' new Galisteo Company could use Edison's process to get rich. Edison himself probably invested a significant amount in the enterprise, though probably not as much as the misleading Burn report suggested he did. In the summer of 1897 Edison prepared a summary of the results of 1896-97 tests on samples from the Ortiz. Edison knew something, or thought he knew.

In 1898 Edison himself visited New Mexico, and was reported by the press as visiting Ortiz in February. While he was here, "Indian Day School", the first movie shot in NM, was filmed at Isleta.

More than a year later Edison sent his chief engineer

---

* A 1970 short historical article was written with a certain amount of sarcasm about Elkins entitled "*New York's First Senator from West Virginia: How Stephen B. Elkins Found a New Political Home*". [West Virginia History 31, January 1970]

Cloyd Chapman and his engineer-brother-in-law John Miller to the old mining camp of Dolores in the Ortiz. They arrived on Feb 9, 1900, and immediately began to build a mill to test the feasibility of the Edison process. The Galisteo Company (the Hoyts) was represented by S.G. Burn, and the landowner, the New Mexico Mining Company, was represented by W.T. Lawson, the son of its then president.

> The Edison mill was constructed a half mile east of Dolores on the edge of Cunningham Mesa, next to Arroyo Viejo, and a couple of hundred yards east of the site of a LAC service building. As the mill building was torn down in 1907 and the foundations were removed around the year 2000, nothing now remains of the Edison mill.

The press covered both Edison's 1898 visit, and the 1900 mill in Dolores as it developed, and Edison was reported as expected at the dedication of the mill in May. When the dedication happened one of the three Hoyt bothers (probably Henry R. Hoyt) was there, and in an oral history taken in 1955 from two surviving mill carpenters (Frank Schmitt and Irving Sweet) Hoyt was probably mistakenly remembered as Edison. Edison was in New Jersey at the time. Only their 55-year-old memories place Edison at the Ortiz mill that day. There is no other evidence that Edison spent the week required for a quick round trip to Cerrillos for the ceremony.

An electrical power line was run from the existing Albemarle generator at Madrid to power the Edison mill, and it was widely reported that at night the mill's electric lights could be seen as far away as Santa Fe.

It is interesting to note that although Burn was an employee of the Galisteo Company, he presented himself to the press as an Edison Laboratory employee. Chapman and Miller reported to Edison that Burn was a problem. He apparently intruded into the construction processs and aggravated carpenters to the brink of quitting. Later in the testing process, Chapman and Miller reported that Burn was unhappy with their gravel sampling. They claimed that Burn would suggest one location and when it did not work out he would claim he told them a different location. With this sense of conflict, frustration, and animosity it is notable that the Census of 1900 indicates that these men were all living in the same domicile.[39]

The first test run of the Edison mill – at this stage, a gravity-and-blower-driven separation process – took place on May 7, 1900. On August 16 Chapman shipped 18 pounds of ore concentrated by this means to Edison in New Jersey. On August 21 Edison commented on the poor quality of the sample. Chapman and Miller, who had surveyed the ore body, reported back to

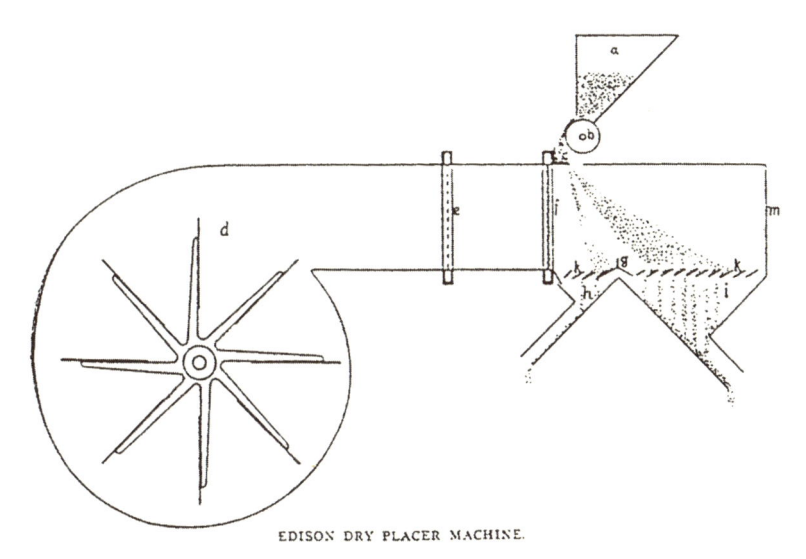

EDISON DRY PLACER MACHINE.

The diagram of Edison's blower-separator aparatus. Left is the electrically-powered blower "d". Top right is the ore hopper "a". Bottom right are the separation screens, the heavier gold-rich material falling into conduit "h" and the lighter waste material into conduit "i".

Edison that there was only enough at Dolores to keep a full-sized mill – if they worked out the problems of clogging screens – in operation for 6 months before exhausting the body, and most of the placer field was below 10 cents per cubic yard, which was the break-even point. These findings were at odds with Burn's earlier assays, and must not have done much to reduce the tension. Chapman and Miller's report meant there was not enough gold to recover projected expenses for the mill.

On October 29, 1900, Edison decided to shut it down, losing his investment. By the end of November 1900 the mill was closed. Edison considered suing the Hoyts for their failure to pay him for the experimental mill at Dolores. In the end Edison paid for it all, although that had not been his intention. [42]

> The separation screens from the Edison gravity-blower mill were recovered and are in existence today, and there are several photographs. The concrete foundation of the mill engine, which is on the south side of Arroyo Viejo a few hundred feet north, of the Cunningham Placer Field, is the only visible remnant of the Edison mill.

On November 19, 1900 W.T. Lawson wrote a personal letter on Galisteo Company, Dolores, N.M., stationery to Edison in New Jersey wherein he uses the phrase, "I have been studying... the Ortiz Grant in order that I might... describe it to one who has not seen it..." He included several photographs for Edison. Either Edison had never seen Dolores, or he hadn't seen the portion where the mill had been built.

The third stage of Edison's dry ore process, as we now know, would have included the use of electromagnets to remove the magnetite from the ore concentrate, further concentrating it. The documentation indicates Edison never sent his electrical apparatus from New Jersey to New Mexico, so only the first two stages, crushing/sorting and gravity separation, were ever perfomed at the Dolores test facility.

The mill building was torn down in 1907 for scrap lumber. In 1909 'a small company' worked the ore body that Chapman and Miller had identified, 2.8 million cubic yards worth, and in 1939-40 the Universal Placer Company finished the job. What Gold Fields Ltd. mined nearly seventy years later was hard rock and much lower quality ore.

In 1903, with Edison's approval, Chapman authored a couple of articles that appeared in both the Engineering & Mining Journal and the Mining World, that described the general outlines of the Edison process, emphasizing the gravity-blower concentrator, and suggesting rights to use the process could be gotten from Edison. There were never any takers.

After 1901 the Hoyts leased sections of placer land and individual mines. They also issued general placer permits for the Ortiz, in return for payment to agents in Golden or Cerrillos of 10% of the gold recovered. By the Depression of the 1930s there were a large number of small-scale placer miners working in the Ortiz Mountains again.

Fayette Jones, writing in 1904, between his two terms as the head of the New Mexico School of Mines, describes the Old Ortiz lode in this way.

"The vein outcropping is an oxidized iron-stained quartz: below the depth of 85 feet the ore becomes base [not acidic], carrying sulphurets of both iron and copper.
"The top portion of the vein was first worked out on account of its free milling qualities." [22]

Jones also lists the then seven current gold lode claims of the Ortiz Mountains: the original Ortiz lode, the Candelaria lode (on the south slope of the Mountains), the Brehm lode (immediately east of and downhill from the Ortiz lode), the Hutchason lode (also on the south slope, on the east side of the Candelaria), the Brown lode (Benton?), the Humbolt 100th lode (which was named to honor the centenary of Alexander von Humbolt's expedition to America), and the new Shoshone lode (1.5 miles north of the Ortiz lode).

⁂

The total estimated Old Placer gold production up from the time of discovery to 1902 is 100,000 ounces. The amount of lode gold produced at Old Placer in this same period is a small part of the overall total, certainly less than the probable error in that estimate. How small was the total lode-mining production? The New Placer figures up to 1959 are somewhat more solid, and they show placer production was six times that of lode production.[24] The placer/lode proportions at Old Placer before the twentieth century may have been about the same: six to one.

The census of 1900, the last enumeration of Dolores, showed nearly the same population as twenty years earlier: 136 people living in 28 houses, 54% of whom had Hispanic surnames. Twenty people stated they were gold miners, and one of those said he was specifically a quartz miner. The inference from the latter job description is that a "gold miner" was probably a placer miner and "quartz miner" a lode miner. Fifteen others specified professions that were related to mining. Still, only 40 % of the adult population of Dolores depended upon mining. There were 48 children 15 years of age or younger.

By 1904 or 1905, around eighty-five years after the first miners had erected their simple shelters in the rocky arroyo below Oso Springs, Dolores was deserted. It was just another New Mexican ghost town.

1905: the last days of Dolores. Looking west. On the right is *Nuestra Señora de los Dolores*. Compare this with the photo on page 113. In the center foreground is the main road to Albuquerque.
Photo by L.C. Graton, courtesy U.S.Geological Survey

The Laboratory of Anthropology of the Museum of New Mexico has designated the site of Dolores town as LA 83571.[33]

The Twentieth Century

Most of the gold mining activity in the first third of the twentieth century was at San Pedro and in New Placer, where large dredges were employed. However, there was some work going on in the Ortiz. The International Mining Manual* for 1911 lists the Ortiz Mine Syndicate, headquartered in Cerrillos, Santa Fe Co., with W. F. Hogan as Manager. "Gold-Silver-Lead. Shafts. Developing."** Mr. Hogan reappears in the same publication from 1914 through 1917, but now as either the Superintendent or General Manager of the Las Norias Mines Co. of Cerrillos, working in the Ortiz Mine Grant, "Placer and Quartz Claims. Developing." The companies were even more ephemeral than the ores.

Charles McKinnis, a California engineer and promoter, leased most of the lode mineral rights in the Ortiz in 1934. In the next five years some preliminary work was done by the Ortiz Gold King Mining Co. at the Old Ortiz mine***, and also a 300-foot shaft was dug at the Mina de Candelaria (on the south side of the Ortiz Mountains), where McKinnis**** constructed a steel hoist frame and some buildings. Neither the Ortiz Gold King nor the Candelaria operations were successful commercially, and there is no record that any ore was milled or shipped from either mine.

The Depression of the 1930s caused an increase in

---

* Alexander R. Dunbar, editor.
** In the parlance of the industry, "developing" means they haven't yet found commercially exploitable quantities of what they were looking for.
*** The Ortiz Gold King Mining Company dewatered and refitted the Old Ortiz mine. The now-shattered headframe timbers near the Santo Niño bat cupola may date from this time. Assays performed on samples obtained in 1936 after the mine was dewatered returned unremarkable results.[42]
**** McKinnis' relationship to the Ortiz Gold King Company is unclear, but the Old Ortiz work appears to be a separate operation from his work at the Candelaria mine.[42]

small-scale placer activity in both placers, and at this time the remaining adobe bricks of old Dolores town were processed for whatever gold was left in them. [64] People got creative. Several old bathtubs found their way into the mountains for water conservation while washing placer sands. [18] During this period much attention was given to the invention and development of a myriad of jigs, drywashing machines, and separation methods for recovery of gold from placers, and the literature describing these techniques is voluminous. [24]

In 1934 President Roosevelt signed the Gold Reserve Act, which stabilized the price of gold at $35 per ounce (just as the Silver Purchase Act fixed silver at 71 cents), and mining in the West began to revive.

In 1939 the Universal Placer Mining Corporation (U.P.M.C.), in a large-scale dry placering operation using draglines, vibrators, and recirculating processes, finished off the last few thousand cubic yards of the placer deposit identified on Cunningham Mesa forty years earlier by Chapman and Miller. Their average recovery rate was 37 cents per cubic yard. U.P.M.C. had closed down operations and was off of Cunningham Mesa by the end of 1939. [66][SANM: Lucien File Collection]

The May 1941 edition of "La Turquesa", the newspaper of Cerrillos High School, contained the following article.

Dry-washing in Progress Again
Beginning July 1, 1940 the Ortiz Grant, under the care of the Galisteo Co., was opened free for dry-washing. Mr. Rosendo Ortiz, representative of the Galisteo Co., gave us figures according to his records. He will issue a permit to anyone in Cerrillos and Madrid. People outside of these towns are not allowed to drywash gold on this grant, except people from Golden and San Pedro. Any person who has this permit can put out any man who

is an outsider. No one is allowed to carry any kind of weapon, to hunt or break down fences. Anyone breaking these rules will not be allowed to dry wash on the grant again.

During the rainy season people are handicapped by the lack of proper machines, which are the only things allowed to get gold with, and they cannot work full time.

Mr. Rosando Ortiz reports that the ground is very wet for dry-washing and no water available for water work, but if it rains hard so the arroyos will flow, he expects this year to be much better than last.

There is no record of numbers of days worked by men, but some made over $4.00 per day. Included was A. Sandoval, who had never turned a wheel on a dry-washer. Others were Ben Martinez, Ben Perea, Carlos Martinez, Rumaldo Ortiz and others. The total income of the four months the men were able to work, was $1,803.79, the average for a week being $150.62.

Wood hauling for the people in Cerrillos is permitted free, but they have to get a permit from Mr. Ortiz the same as for dry washing. This permit is good for one load of wood at a time only. Permits will be issued any time they are needed provided they gather dead wood only.

[La Turquesa Vol.IX No.5, May 1941; Frank Sandoval, Teddy Perea eds.]

The U.S. government issued a series of regulations in 1942 that were designed to redirect all labor and resources to fighting World War II. One of them, War Board Order L-208, shut down all gold mines for the duration. In addition, metal salvage operations during World War II caused much of the machinery and evidence of industrial workings in and around the Ortiz area to be removed, [64] devastating the infrastructure of the mines. Many miners and prospectors left the field for the cities and never returned. When the war finally ended the strong post-war dollar and low price of gold combined to keep many of the mines closed.

The Hoyts (the Galisteo Company) sold the Ortiz Mining Grant to the U.S. government in 1941, but the lawsuits necessary to clear the title from the New Mexico Mining Company delayed that transfer for two

**Ortiz Mine Grant
Sections & Subdivisions**

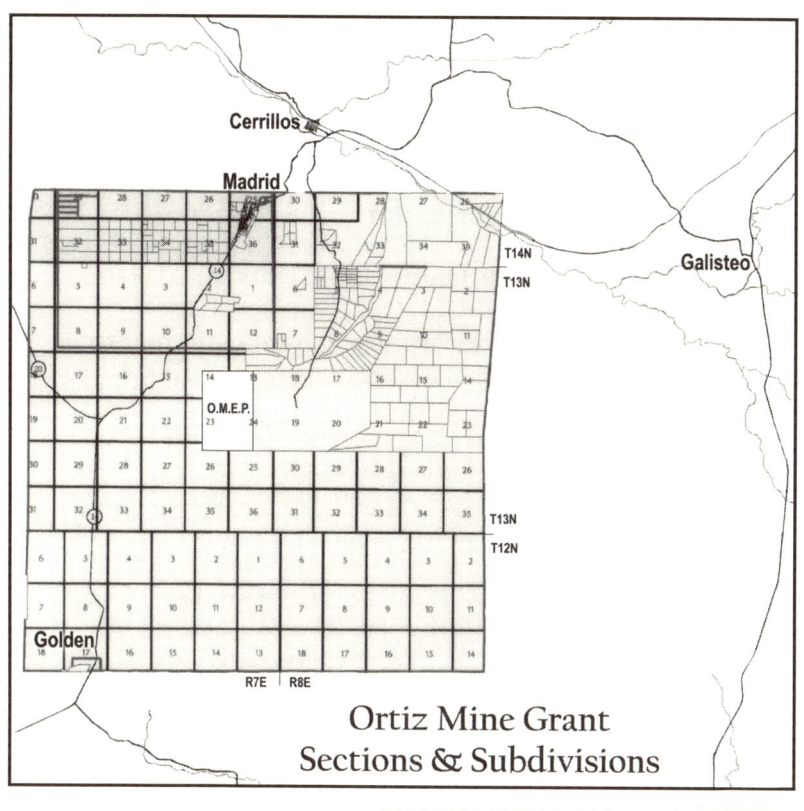

Gil Griswold's Ortiz Mines
Company office in Golden.

J.K. Shishkin Photograph Collection #0181
New Mexico State Archives Image#2398

years. The courts in the meantime placed the N.M.M.C. into receivership. The sale was finally consummated on June 24, 1943 when the Ortiz Cooperative Livestock Association (a government financed cooperative), using funds from the U.S. Farm Security Administration, acquired the property for grazing purposes. The Ortiz Cooperative Livestock Association never made any of its mortgage payements, and they were placed in default in 1946, when the grant was sold again, this time at auction. At that auction there was only one bidder; Mrs. George W. Potter of Joplin, Missouri. She paid approximately $125,000 for the property.

The next year (February 1947) the new owners, Mr. and Mrs. Potter, sold the bulk of the Ortiz Grant surface rights to Howell Gage, W. L. McDonald and Frank Young. The Potters retained the mineral rights to the entire grant, and within a year had purchased additionally the surface rights to five small areas (the exceptions to the Hoyt's 1900 lease of the Ortiz Mine Grant: four on the south slope of the mountains and one on the north slope; Exception #5, the New Live Oak claim, is a short distance east of the Preserve).

Since 1947 the surface ownership in the northern part of the Ortiz Grant has been sold and resold many times, until today it is divided into a great number of parcels.* The southern portion of the Ortiz Grant remains in a few rather large ranch tracts, the largest being Howell Gage's Lone Mountain Ranch.

The Ortiz Mines Company (O.M.C) of Joplin, Missouri, was formed by George W. and Emily W. Potter and Frank Simms (who lived in Miami, Oklahoma) to manage the Ortiz mineral rights. To assist in the development of the Ortiz minerals in 1946 O.M.C.

---

* The primary access to the majority of these old northside Ortiz Grant parcels is County Road 55, Goldmine Road.

hired Clyde T. Griswold, a retired mining engineer for the A.T.&S.F., to map the Grant, and his son, Gil R. Griswold, to function as O.M.C. agent.

C. T. Griswold's map was completed by 1950. Agent Gil Griswold's O.M.C. office was initially in Golden, but by 1948 he and the office took over much of the ground floor of the old Palace Hotel in Cerrillos, where he continued to live until leaving the company in 1956.

Griswold's responsibilities at the mines included managing a crew of fifteen to eighteen workers who dug test shafts and explored the old mines for possible ores (in the mid 1950s building a new headframe for the Benton shaft south of the Cunningham Mine). Griswold built the Potter-Simms laboratory building at the old Las Norias mill site, and used it for the assay of the placer and lode samples obtained by his crew, and the storage of records.[18]

> The site occupied by the Potter-Simms building, the "Lower Mill" of Dolores, has been given the Laboratory of Anthropology number 87601.

Griswold said that at this time he "did lots of work on [a deposit of diffuse gold and tungsten at] Cunningham Hill", and he recalled that not often, but more than once, Dolores Arroyo flooded him out of the lab building.[18] The laboratory structure, though somewhat run down today, still survives.

The Silas Mason Company of New York obtained a mineral lease from the Potters (O.M.C.) and did a considerable amount of placer sampling and prospecting in 1946 and 1947.

Between 1950 and 1970, in the hopes of garnering a lucrative mineral project, O.M.C. invited additional companies to do geologic evaluations in the Ortiz.

Many responded. In those two decades there were approximately 50 different evaluations performed. [42]

Paul Roberson operated a ranch in the Ortiz from 1953 to 1974. The building that served as Roberson's home and as the ranch headquarters is still standing on the west side of the arroyo through the Dolores townsite, and may preserve some of the walls of José Francisco Ortiz' home and store built a hundred and twenty years before. As to the location of Ortiz' house, there is some contrary evidence – a Dolores map from the 1860s shows the N.M.M.C. mill on that site – so this connection to the original Ortiz *tienda* may be no more than a well-promoted myth. [42]

Gold Fields and LAC

In 1972 Gold Fields Ltd., an international company headquartered in South Africa, after test drilling in the Cunningham deposit, leased 36,000 acres of mineral rights from the Ortiz Mines Company and purchased another 4,300 acres outright. Their Cunningham Mine was situated on a breccia-filled volcanic vent, 400 by 700 feet in size at the surface, in some parts of which geological hydrothermal activity had concentrated gold.

Between 1980 and 1987, using a three-stage crusher and the batch or heap cyanide-leach process, Gold Fields completely extracted the large ore body, moving 25 million tons of rock in the process, [18] and producing (officially) 231,900 troy ounces of gold. The figure of 250,000 troy ounces is commonly given, and may be closer to the truth. This was two-and-a-half times return on capital investment over about eight years' time, and represents significantly over half of the estimated total gold production, both placer and lode, for all of the Ortiz Mountains over the previous 160 years. Over half of 160 years' worth of gold production in only eight years!

The former location of this large ore body is a 385-foot deep open pit, now slowly filling with water.

Gold Fields ranged widely over their 40,300 acres looking for additional gold. Most of the long, deep, prospect trenches in and near the Preserve were bulldozed at this time. Gold Fields also removed and processed much of the downslope waste material from the Old Ortiz mine site, pushing those rims (see page 49) off to the side.

Gold is extracted from crushed gold-bearing quartz by forming a complex with sodium cyanide.

$$4\ Au + 8\ NaCN + H_2O + O_2 \Longrightarrow 4\ NaOH + 4\ NaAu(CN)_2$$

One option for recovery of the gold from the complex is by precipitation with zinc dust.

$$NaAu(CN)_2 + Zn \Longrightarrow Na_2Zn(CN)_2 + 2\ Au$$

The term for the final sodium-zinc-cyanide-gold mixture is "pregnant solution". In the above equation the gold is extracted from the pregnant solution with zinc dust. Another option for final recovery might be to roast the pregnant solution in the presence of a flux such as borax. The resulting metallic gold button may contain ten percent or more silver. [5]

Gold Fields chose yet a third method of recovering the gold from the pregnant solution; electroplating it onto stainless steel. Their recovery of gold from the Cunningham Mine ore was greater than 90 percent. [40]

During this time (June 30, 1985) the largest armed robbery in New Mexico history took place, when robbers tied up the guards and took $313,000 in gold from the plating plant at Dolores. "It appears as though they knew what they were doing.... They knew where everything was." [Santa Fe New Mexican, 6-30-83] Indeed they did. The subsequent arrests recovered most of the gold.

When in 1979 Gold Fields began work at the Cunningham Mine, gold was selling for more than $700 per ounce. By 1984 gold was less than $350 an ounce. The following year, at the time of its announcement of the impending shutdown, Gold Fields stated that the mine had been unprofitable since 1984.

View, looking west, of the Cunningham Deposit. The open pit, lower center, is slowly filling with water. The reverse osmosis treatment ponds, above and to the right, are on top of the waste-rock dump. The Old Ortiz mine is in the distance, at the left edge of this photo. The peaks are within the O.M.E.P.
Photo 2000, from author's collection.

Two years after Gold Fields shut down the Cunningham mine, Pegasus Gold Corporation entered into a joint venture (the Ortiz Joint Venture) with LAC Minerals U.S.A., which had in the interim acquired the Gold Fields Ltd./Ortiz Mines Company mineral lease. Between 1989 and 1992 Pegasus mapped out two ore bodies on the south side of the Ortiz Mountains above two old Mexican placer fields (in Lukas and Carache canyons) with 500,000 ounces of proven reserves.

In August 1991 an "acid rock drainage problem" was identified at the waste rock dump of the old Gold Fields' Cunningham Hill mine.

Acid rock drainage (ARD) is water pollution formed when rocks containing sulfides, in this case primarily pyrites or "fool's gold", are exposed to air and water. The water passing over those rocks becomes acidic, enabling it to dissolve heavy metals and nonmetal constituents from the rocks it comes in contact with. As recently as 2003 the State of New Mexico Environment Department (NMED) identified levels of aluminum, cadmium, sulfate, iron, manganese and total dissolved solids in the upper Dolores Gulch water which exceed New Mexico ground water quality standards.[45] Acid rock drainage is dangerous to both plants and animals.

The Dolores Gulch ARD (Acid Rock Drainage) discovery led to additional findings of mining-related pollution. Acid water was filling the open pit – created by the same pyrites-air-water chemistry as the waste pile ARD. A plume of cyanide and nitrates (nitrates are a decomposition product of cyanide) appeared in the groundwater beneath the large leachate residue pile on the east side. Since about 1985, when Gold Fields had referred to it as only a "minor" problem, the companies had been pumping the contaminated plume water there out of the ground and treating it. But now it was clear things were worse than people had been led to believe.

In 1990 Jeanie Cragin and others founded the Friends of Santa Fe County (F.S.F.C.). This citizens' group was originally created in response to a Pegasus Gold and Placer Dome corporations proposal to construct new gold mines in the Ortiz Mountains and Cerrillos Hills. Placer Dome's Cerrillos project was abandoned in late 1990.

The efforts of the F.S.F.C. were instrumental in the creation of the Santa Fe County Mining Ordinance of 1991.

In 1992 the Friends of Santa Fe County met numerous times with representatives of Gold Fields, Pegasus and LAC to discuss the needed reclamation at the Cunningham Hill Mine and possible controls on future mining elsewhere in the Ortiz. The companies were not receptive to the suggestions of the Friends.[15] In the same year F.S.F.C. obtained the assistance of the New Mexico Environmental Law Center (Doug Meiklejohn, Executive Director), and in 1994 Doug Wolf of the Law Center filed a lawsuit on behalf of FSFC against Gold Fields, Pegasus and LAC over the pollution and damage to the environment.

In 1992, after expending a very large amount of money – $19 million is one of the numbers put forth – and faced with growing local and regional opposition to the open pit/cyanide leach pile procedure, Pegasus Gold Corporation withdrew from the joint venture, leaving LAC Minerals alone to pursue the project. Pegasus ultimately filed reorganization bankruptcy in January 1998, walked away from all its underperforming mines and many of its environmental disasters, and re-emerged as Apollo Gold Corporation by which name it is known today.

LAC was acquired by the Canadian international Barrick Gold Corporation in 1994, where it is currently managed as a corporate division.

In June 1995 LAC, as the surviving partner of the joint venture, announced it was abandoning plans to mine gold in the Ortiz Mountains, and that it intended to settle the lawsuit as well. An agreeable settlement was successfully completed on May 23, 1996, and the lawsuit* was, with the agreement of both parties, dismissed from court. The settlement stipulated that LAC would develop, through negotiations with F.S.F.C., a reclamation plan for the area, and LAC would also donate the western third of its holdings to an appropriate nonprofit organization. It took seven years of work (with important participation by Tom Parker, Doug

---

* Friends of Santa Fe County et al. v. LAC Minerals (U.S.A.) et al.

Wolf, Jeanie Cragin, Val Green and Art Montana), but in the end the New Mexico State Environment Department and the Mining and Minerals Division accepted LAC's closeout and other reclamation plans. [15]

In April of 2001 the Santa Fe Botanical Garden, through the Santa Fe Trust for Public Lands, accepted from LAC Minerals (U.S.A.) the donation of 1,350 acres in the western portion of their holdings, which comprises all of the higher mountain peaks.

The long-term solution to the ARD into the open pit is to submerge the exposed sulfides by allowing the pit to fill with water, a process that is expected to take about 60 years. By mid 2003, after 16 years of natural inflow, the water in the 385-foot deep open pit was at the 118-foot level. The pit will continue to be monitored, and treated with lime (to reduce acidity and precipitate dissolved metals) and/or reverse osmosis (to reduce the level of specific contaminants) whenever water quality fails to meet NMED standards. [45]

The eastside groundwater cyanide-nitrate plume is expected to meet NMED standards within the next few years, but the monitoring of groundwater there will continue. Final remediation at the groundwater plume is expected within the next ten years. [45]

As for the waste pile problem south of the Dolores townsite, near the original Ojo del Oso – the place where it all began nearly two hundred years ago – the volume of ARD water has recently been significantly decreased, but acidic water will continue to flow out of that waste pile for decades to come.

In the words of F.S.F.C. advisor and Environmental

Consultant Art Montana, "LAC Minerals should be recognized for their extraordinary efforts in reclaiming Cunningham Hill. All inhabitants of Santa Fe County must be thankful for LAC's commitment to carry out the remediation using the best available procedures." [15]

O. M. E. P.

In late summer 2002 the Santa Fe Botanical Garden's Ortiz Mountains Educational Preserve was formally dedicated. The year also saw the enlistment and training of a cadre of volunteer docents.

For most of the summer and fall of 2002 the New Mexico State Abandoned Mine Land Bureau (A.M.L.) sponsored a project to safeguard the seventeen most hazardous mine shafts. Two of the seventeen mines are inhabited by bat colonies, primarily Townsend's Big-eared bats. A.M.L. stabilized the Tunia shaft of the old Santo Niño, which had suffered on its northern side from substantial caving, and capped the main shaft with a steel bat cupola. The second bat cupola is to the east of the Preserve on LAC property. Other deep shafts and pits in the immediate area have been filled or fenced.

Upon the 2003 completion of the mine hazards abatement project came the first of what are expected to be many, many regular public excursions into the Ortiz Mountains Educational Preserve. The Preserve also serves as a laboratory for naturalists, historians, geologists and other academics, as well as an outdoor classroom open to all the students of New Mexico.

For two hundred years people were drawn to the Ortiz for all possible reasons. But whether it be debt or love or salvation or adventure or greed, in the final analysis they came to the Ortiz Mountains for only one thing. They came for the gold.

When you visit the Preserve you will see all around you the rusting and crumbling relics of their time here. Most obvious are the thousands of late nineteenth-century and twentieth-century rusting metal cans.

> Examine the can. If the vertical seam shows lead solder, it produced between 1847 and 1870. If the top of the can (on either a large hole or a pin prick) shows a solder seal it is from 1819 to 1930. After inspecting cans and other artifacts, please carefully return them to their original locations. Remember, this is an educational PRESERVE.

You may see a square nail or a piece of broken bottle, a ground stone or a piece of a red brick, or part of an old harmonica. If you look closely among the piñons and low oaks you will see the outlines of the small, flat tent pads and lean-to alcoves, perhaps even the one once used by Dolores Jalomo himself.

Occasionally among the trees you will see an old axe-cut or saw-cut stump. Did that tree go for shoring up a mine? Or framing a tent, or as a viga in an adobe building? For the steam-powered saw mill? Or fuel for a cooking fire? Was it cut down fifty years ago or two hundred? It's your guess.

If you find a really secluded spot and sit very quietly with your eyes closed, you just might be touched by the spirit of *el Padre mina,* and the old man may bless you with a vision of the great and fabled galleries of solid gold that lie somewhere deep beneath your feet, somewhere within the mountains that bear the name of Señor Don José Francisco Ortiz.

To visit the Preserve, or for more information, contact the Santa Fe Botanical Garden, P.O. Box 23343, Santa Fe, NM 87502-3343, or call (505) 428-1684.

Acknowledgments

I would like to thank all of you who made this book possible, but a few of you need special recognition. And one remarkable person looms large on this list. Homer Milford was recently severely chided by his boss – I'm assuming you're going to stay retired now, Homer, so this story is safe? – because of his Google *curriculum vitae*. He couldn't possibly accumulate so many Google references and at the same time be tending to business. Yes, he could! A mild mannered biologist by day, Homer was and is THE major clearing house for the mining history of New Mexico, and the single most important impetus for this book. Thank you Homer.

Fred Leckman, who doesn't know it, but you got me going again, and you pointed me to Gil Griswold. Thank you.

Thanks to Charles Strom of White City, Kansas, for sharing the American life of Charlie Parker.

Heartfelt thanks go to the many good people of the Santa Fe Botanical Garden, who have the great fortune to steward the remarkable and unique Ortiz Mountains Educational Preserve, and who share it with the world. Many thanks go also to the S.F.B.G.'s indefatigable and *sui generis* Todd Brown, the O.M.E.P. man who not quite single-handedly (Where would he be without Patricia?) does everything there. Sui, Todd!

And to Ardeth Baxter and Pam Christie, editors extraordinaire who bent but didn't break my stylistic eccentricities. The only conceivable source for an error or typo in this book is one of my unredacted rewrites.

And finally, thanks go to Jeanie Cragin. In this case the analogy of birthing might be appropriate. You never know at the time how it's going to turn out. Jeanie, the Ortiz Mountains Educational Preserve turned out just fine.

Sources

1 - Lt. James W. Abert, *Expedition to the Southwest. An 1845 Reconnaissance of Colorado, New Mexico, Texas, and Oklahoma*, University of Nebraska Press, Lincoln, Nebraska, 1999

2 - D.E. Alberts (Ed), *Rebels on the Rio Grande: The Civil War Journal of A.B. Peticolas*, UNM Press, 1984

3 - R. Arnold, *The Ortiz Mine Grant, New Mexico*, A June 20, 1933 Memorandum

4 - Adolph Bandelier, 1892, John Meredith, trans.

5 - Garnet Basque, *Gold Panner's Manual*, Sunfire Publictions Ltd, 1991

6 - W.A. Bell, *New Tracks in North America. A Journal of Travel and Adventure Whilst Engaged in the Survey for a Southern Railroad to the Pacific Ocean During 1867-68*, Schibner, Welford, New York, 1870

7 - J.J. Bowden, *Private Land Claims in the Southwest*, Master's thesis, SMU, 1969

8 - E. Boyd, *Popular Arts of Spanish New Mexico*, Museum of New Mexico Press, Santa Fe, 1974

9 - Paige Christiansen, *The Story of Mining in New Mexico. Scenic Trips to the Geological Past, No. 12, New Mexico Bureau of Mines and Mineral Resources*, Socorro, 1974.
[Though replete with numerous colorful references that have been widely reproduced and cited elsewhere, this book is little used in this paper because of imputations of unreliability and insufficient rigor.]

10 - Jill K. Cliburn, personal communication, 2003
["Kirt (Kempter) [said] that the Ortiz was probably twice the size it is today, and that the main feature was a giant volcano— "think Mount Fuji," he said. It is impossible to say how many explosive eruptions there were, but we know it was a very active site."]

11 - David Dary, *The Santa Fe Trail, Its History, Legends & Lore*, Penguin Books, 2000

12 - Jane Lenz Elder & David J. Weber, *Trading in Santa Fe, John M. Kingsbury's Correspondence with James Josiah Webb, 1853-1861*, Southern Methodist University Press, Dallas, 1996

13 - Letter from Samuel Ellison to Col. A. B. Carey, Jan. 13, 1866, pp 20-21, *Compleation of Facts, San Pedro & Canyon del Agua Grants*, Washinton D.C., 1867

14 - Robert W. Frazer, *Forts and Supplies, The Role of the Army in the Economy of the Southwest, 1846-1861*, UNM Press, Albuquerque, 1983

15 - *GREEN FIRE REPORT*, A Publication of the New Mexico Environmental Law Center, Santa Fe, Summer 1996

16 - Josiah Gregg, *Commerce of the Prairies* [1844], Southwestern Press, Dallas, 1933

17 - John Greiner, *The Private Letters of A Government Official in the Southwest*, transcribed by Tod B. Galloway, in The Journal of American History, vol.3, 1909

18 - Gil Griswold, personal communication June 29, 2003

19 - Charles W. Hackett; *Historical Documents Relating to New Mexico, Nueva Viscaya, and Approaches Thereto, to 1773*, collected by A&F Bandelier, Carnegie Institution of Washington, D.C., 1937

20 - Hammond & Ray, Viceregal summary entitled "*True Report Drawn from the Letters, Statements, and Papers which Governor Don Juan de Oñate Enclosed with His Letter of March 22, 1601, Addressed to His Brothers and Relatives*".1953

21 - Paul Horgan, *Great River, The Rio Grande in North American History*, Wesleyan University Press, 1984

22 - Fayette Jones, *New Mexico Mines and Minerals, 1904*, reprinted in Old Mines and Ghost Camps of New Mexico by Frontier Book Co., Fort Davis, TX, 1968

23 - Calvin Horn, *New Mexico's Troubled Years. The Story of the Early Territorial Governors*, Horn & Wallace, Albuquerque, 1963

24 - Maureen G. Johnson, *Placer Gold Deposits of New Mexico*, US DOI Geological Survey Bulletin 1348, reprinted by Gem Guides Book Co, 1992

25 - George W. Julian, "Land-Stealing in New Mexico," *The North American Review*, vol. CXLV, No. 368, pp. 2- 31, 1885

26 - William A. Keleher, *Turmoil in New Mexico 1846-1868*, Rydal Press, Santa Fe, 1952

27 - Moses Kelly, *Preliminary Report (Ortiz Mine Grant) for Use of New Mexico Mining Company Stockholders*, Baker & Goodwin, New York, 1864

28 - R.E. Kelly & M.C.S. Kelly, *Arrastras, Unique Western Historic Mining Sites*, In HISTORICAL ARCHAEOLOGY 17:1, 1983

29 - John L. Kessell, *Kiva, Cross & Crown*, Southwest Parks & Monuments Association, Tucson, 1987, p.317

30 - ___ *Spain in the Southwest*, University of Oklahoma Press, Norman, 2002

31 - *LAND OF SUNSHINE*, compiled and edited by Max. Frost & Paul A.F. Walter, Santa Fe, NM, 1906

32 - Ruth Laughlin, *The Wind Leaves No Shadow*, The Caxton Printers Ltd, Caldwell, ID, 1948. [Ms. Laughlin's fictional account offers a colorful and useful portrayal of the daily life of ordinary people in nineteenth century Real de Dolores and northern New Mexcio. This book, however, contains some significant chronological and historical errors.]

33 - Daisy F. Levine & Linda J. Goodman, *An Archaeological and Ethnohistoric Survey within the Cerrillos Mining District, Santa Fe County, New Mexico*, Laboratory of Anthropology Note No.508, 1990

34 - W.W. Long, *A History of Mining in New Mexico During the Spanish and Mexican Periods*, Master's thesis, UNM, 1964

35 - Charles Lummis, *Letters from the Southwest*, James W. Byrkit, Ed., University of Arizona Press, 1989

36 - J.D. Meketa, *Legacy of Honor: The Life of Rafael Chacon, A Nineteenth-Century New Mexican*, UNM, 1986

37 - David Meriwether, *My Life in the Mountains and on the Plains*, University of Oklahoma Press, Norman, reprint 1965

38 - Will Meyerriecks, *Drills and Mills: Precious Metal Mining and Milling Methods of the Frontier West*, Tampa, FL, 2001

39 - Homer E. Milford, *Thomas A. Edison's Dry Placer Mill at Dolores, New Mexico*, Third International Mining History Conference, Boulder, CO, June, 1994

40 - ___ *Mining History of the Cunningham Deposit and Ortiz Mine Grant, Santa Fe County, New Mexico*, in New Mexico Geological Society Guidebook, 46th Field Conference, Geology of the Santa Fe Region, 1995

41 - ___ *Real De Dolores. Nomination for the Mining History Association's Year of Mining and Historic Preservation*, 1999

42 - ___ personal communication, July-December 2003

43 - *THE MINES OF NEW MEXICO*, by the New Mexico Bureau of Immigration, 1896 May

44 - Jill Mocho, *Murder & Justice in Frontier New Mexico 1821 - 1846*, UNM Press, 1997

45 - New Mexico Environment Department, Memorandum, September 29, 2003, *Cunningham Hill Mine Reclamation Success*, Jeff Sanders, Geologist, Ground Water Quality Bureau

46 - Rosemary Nusbaum, *Tierra Dulce, Reminiscences from the Jesse Nusbaum Papers*, The Sunstone Press, Santa Fe, 1980

47 - T.M. Pearce (Ed.), *New Mexico Place Names, A Geographical Dictionary*, UNM Press, 1965

48 - R.W. Raymond, *Statistics of Mines and Mining in the States and Territories for the Year 1869*, Executive Document No.54 40th Congress 3rd Session, U.S. Government Printing Office, 1870

49 - ___ *Statistics of Mines and Mining in the States and Territories West of the Rocky Mountains: Being the Sixth Annual Report*, 43rd Congress, 1st Session, House of Representatives Executive Document No.141, U.S. Government Printing Office, 1874

50 - Carroll Riley, *Rio del Norte*, University of Utah Press, 1995
[p.169; At Cicuye in 1540 Bigotes regales Coronado with tales of gold in the lands to the east.]

51 - ____ *The Kachina and the Cross*, University of Utah Press, 1999

52 - Santa Fe County Records, *Locations & Mining Deeds*, New Mexico Records Center and Archives, Santa Fe.

53 - *Santa Fe Weekly New Mexican*, newspaper, Santa Fe, NM

54 - Marc Simmons, *Turquoise and Six Guns*, The Sunstone Press, Santa Fe, 1993

55 - *Spanish Archives of New Mexico*, Land Office Records, New Mexico Records Center and Archives, Santa Fe. Original Spanish documents on land titles. (WPATSA: transla-

tions by Work Progress Administration).

56 - *Dr. M. Steck Collection*, University of New Mexico, Albuquerque

57 - John E. Sunder, *Matt Field on the Santa Fe Trail*, Collected by Clyde and Mae Reed Porter, Univ. of Oklahoma Press, 1960

58 - *Surveyor General Reports*, New Mexico State Records Center and Archives, Santa Fe.

59 - Alfred Barnaby Thomas, *Forgotten Frontiers: A Study of the Spanish Indian Policy of Don Juan Bautista de Anza Governor of New Mexico, 1777-1778*. University of Oklahoma Press, Norman, 1932, p.112

60 - Robert J. Torres, *The Risks of Business, Round the Roundhouse - Voices from the Past* (newspaper column), Santa Fe, 1999

61 - John M. Townley, *Mining in the Ortiz Mine Grant Area, Southern Santa Fe County, New Mexico*, Master's thesis, University of Nevada, Reno, 1967

62 - ___ *The New Mexico Mining Company*, The New Mexico Historical Review, vol.46, 1971

63 - ___ *History of the Ortiz Grant Mining Region, Santa Fe County, New Mexico*, Great Basin Studies Center, n.d. [early-mid 1990s] [It is reported that this short paper was hurriedly produced, which possibly explains its numerous errors and confabulations. There are few references to this document within this report.]

64 - TRC Mariah Associates Inc., David P. Staley Principal Investigator, *Real de Dolores, The History and Archaeology of New Mexico's First Gold Rush Town*, NMCRIS Project Number 55157, 1997

65 - Ralph Emerson Twitchell, *The Leading Facts of New Mexico History*, Horn & Wallace, Albuquerque, 1963

66 - ___ *Spanish Archives of New Mexico*, Reprint by Arno Press, New York, 1976

67 - Frederick Adolphus Wislizneus, M.D., *Memoir of a Tour of Northern Mexico, Connected with Colonel Doniphan's Expedition in 1846 and 1847*, U.S. Senate, Miscellaneous Documents, No. 26, 30th Congress, 1st Session. Reprinted by Rio Grande Press, Glorieta, 1969, and Calvin Horn Publishers, Albuquerque, 1969

68 - WPATSA, Work Progress Administration Translation of Spanish Archives

INDEX

Abandoned Mine Land Bureau, 13, 59, 91, 138
Abert, Lieut., 55, 61-62
Abiquiú, 39
Abreú, Marcelino, 41, 45
Abreú, Roman, 35, 37-39
Abreú, Santiago, 45
Abreú, Soledad, 70
acid rock drainage (ARD), 133-136
adobe bricks, 125
Aguilar, Luís, 57
Alamo Creek, 87
Albemarle, 118
Albuquerque, 94, 108, 123
alcalde, 16, 24, 39-42, 45, 57
Alejo, Rafael, 38-39, 65
Alvarez, Manuel, 50
amalgam, 10, 22, 47, 63, 97
amalgamation, 10, 21-22, 110
Anderson, Col. A. L., 85, 98-99
Anton Chico, 75
ants, 71
Apollo Gold Corporation, 135
argentum, 22
Arizona, 82
Armijo, Governor, 39, 52, 54
Armijo, Nestor, 41
Arny, acting governor, 82
arrastra, 10, 17, 21, 46-49, 57, 62, 72, 79-80, 86
artesian wells, 92
Atchison, Topeka & Santa Fe R.R. (A.T. & S.F.), 95, 104, 107-108, 111-112, 116, 128
Austro-Hungary, 112
azogue, 22

Baca y Ortiz, Francisco, 40, 42-43
Baca y Terrus, José Francisco, 35
bathtubs, 124
Barceló, Gertrudis (see Tules), 24, 36
Barceló, Trinidad, 36, 57
Barela y Borrego, Salvador, 51-53
barra, 10, 19
Barrick Gold Corporation, 135
bat cupola, 12-13, 42, 124, 138
batea, batia, 9-10, 21, 31, 33

Beaubien, Carlos, 49, 66
Beck, Preston Jr., 75
Becknell, Capt. William, 27, 30
Bell, Willam A., 97
beneficio, 23
Benton (Benson) lode, 122, 129
Bernalillo, 76
Big Ditch, 89
Blake, William P., 70-71
Blanco, Pueblo, 2
borax, 132
Bosque Redondo, 84
breccia, 5, 131
Brehm lode, 98, 116, 122
Brown lode, 122
Brown, Todd, 49
Burn, Samuel G., 117-118
buscones, 31

California, 50-51, 57, 64, 124
Camino Real, el, 24, 26
Canada, Canadian, 56, 135
Candelaria lode (*la mina*), 122, 124
Cano, Ignacio, 38-45, 49-50, 65-66, 77, 110
Captain Davis Mt., 3, 88, 95
Carache Canyon, 133
Carbonateville (settlement), 21
Carey, Lt. Col. A. B., 86
Carlos III, King, 11
Carleton, Gen. James H., 84, 86
Carpenter, H. H., 108
Carondelet Company, 70, 72-73, 79
Catron, Thomas B., 78, 82, 89, 102-106
Cedar Mt., 3
Census, 100-101, 114, 119, 122
Cerrillos Coal & Iron Company, 104, 109, 111
Cerrillos Coal Rail Road Company, 112, 116
Cerrillos, El Real de los, 16
Cerrillos Hills, 4, 11, 15, 21-23, 29, 37, 103, 134
Cerrillos, Los, 87, 105
Cerrillos Rustler, 115
Cerrillos Station, 95, 107-108
Chacón, Governor, 18

- 148 -

Chacón, José Albino, 61
Chacón, Rafael, 61
Chaffee, Jerome B., 99, 102, 106, 109
Chamuscado, Capt., 15
Chapman, Cloyd, 118-121, 125
Chávez, Gov. José Antonio, 113
Chihuahua (province), 30, 36, 39
Chihuahua (city), 4, 25-26, 28-29, 52, 57, 76
Chilean (Chillian) mill, 47, 71
Civil War, 48, 58, 67, 70, 80-82, 84, 89, 104
Clancy, Harry S., 106
Clark, William, 7
Clifton, Arizona, 89
Coal Bank, 80, 109
colorado (mineral), 20
Colorado, 72, 103, 106
Compromiso, mina de, 44
Connelly, Dr. Henry, 75-76
Consolidated Land, Cattle Raising & Wool Growing Company, 105
Cook, Captain, 39
Cooper, Stephen, 28
Coronado, 3, 15
Coryell, Lewis S., 75
coyote shafts, 13
Cox, E. T., 83
Cox, J. D., 103
Cragin, Jeanie, 134-136
cuña, 10, 19
Cunningham deposit (mine), 44, 60, 111, 120, 129, 131-133
Cunningham, Maj. Francis A., 75-76
Cunningham gulch, 5, 6, 76
Cunningham Hill, 95, 129, 137
Cunningham Mesa, 111, 118, 125
cyanide, 110, 131-136

Daily, Andrew W., 51
Dallum, Richard, 56
Dary, David, 30, 53
Davis, Capt. N.S., 89, 92-93, 96
decline (mine tunnel), 42, 90-92, 93
deep placering, 10, 21
Deer Spring, 34, 46
Delgado, Felipe S., 84
Delgado, Fernando, 39, 45
Delgado, Manuel S., 35, 37, 41, 49, 66, 84
Delgado, mina de, 37

denounce (a mine), 8, 11-12, 16, 37-38, 87
Denver, Colorado, 102
Depression, The, 121, 124
descubridora, 40
diamond mine, 14
diatreme, 5
Dolores Arroyo, 129
Dolores, el Real de, 2, 23, 34, (first use) 38, 40-41, 45, 65, 92, 95, 112
Dolores del Oro, 51, 53, 113
Dolores Gulch, 6, 62, 134
Domingo, 107
Dorsey, Stephen W., 103
dry placer, 6, 21
dry, drywashing machine, 124-126
Dunbar, Alexander, 124
Durango, 54

echadero, 10
Edgewood, 4
Edison, Thomas, 20, 117-120
El Dorado, 15
El Paso, 31, 80
electroplating, 132
Elkins, Samuel H., 111, 116
Elkins, Stephen B., 69, 78, 82, 99, 102-106, 109-112, 117
Elizabethtown, 89
Ellison, Samuel, 79-82, 86
Ellsworth, Kansas, 88
emeralds, 11
Emmert, W. M., 114
Engineering and Mining Journal, 121
Entrada, 15
Escalante, Felipe de, 15
Escalante, las minas de, 15
escalera, 11
Españole, 26
Espinaso Formation, 5
estancas, 33
Exceptions (to the Ortiz Grant), 128

Faraon Apaches, 17
Federal Place, 53
Felipe IV (King of Spain), 36
Flores, Governor, 17
Fort Union, 80
Franklin, Missouri, 27
free milling, 21, 69, 96, 99-100, 114, 121
Friends of Santa Fe County, 134-136

Gage, Howell, 128
galena, 15
Galisteo Company, 117-120, 124-126
Galisteo Junction, 108
Galisteo River (Creek), 5, 18, 87, 95, 108
Garcia, José de Jésus, 38-39, 65
Garcia, Juana, 51
Geronimo, A., 87
Gildersleeve, Charles H., 78
Gold Fields Ltd., 44, 60, 121, 131-135
Gold Reserve Act of 1934, 125
Golden (settlement), 15, 17, 34, 59, 95, 101, 114, 121, 125, 126-129
Goldmine Road, 5, 128
Grant, Ulysses S., 82, 108
Gregg, Josiah, 30, 46, 50, 53, 60
Greiner, John, 40, 64-67, 69, 82, 84, 87-88, 111
Greiner, Theodore S., 87
Green, Val, 136
Griffith, D. W., 112
Griswold, Clyde T., 129
Griswold, Gil R., 127-129
grizzly bear, 56

Haines, Hiram, 100
Hart, Robert, 103
hematite, 20
Hersch, Joseph, 73, 79
highgrading, 32
Hoan, Doc, 74
Hogan, W. F., 124
hombre bueno, 39
Hoyt brothers, 102, 104, 114, 116-121, 128
Hoyt, Henry R., 118
Humbolt 100th lode, 122
Hutchason lode, 122

Idler, William, 71-75
"Indian Day School", 117
Indiana State University, 82
International Mining Manual, 124
iron, 55, 71, 92-93, 96, 99, 121, 134
Isleta (Pueblo), 116

Jacobs, Sarah, 102
Jalomo, Dolores, 8, 11, 12, 35, 37-38, 41, 43, 45-46, 139
James, Thomas, 27

James and Condict patent, 88
Janos Presidio, 36
Jefferson, Thomas, 7
Johnson, Maureen G., 6, 59
Jones, Prof. Fayette A., 14, 121-122
Jones, Fred W., 88
Joplin, Missouri, 128
Juez de Paz, 52
Julian, George W., 78

Kansas City, 85, 88
Kansas City Journal, 108
Kansas River, 7
Kearny, General, 53, 61
Kelly, Moses, 78, 83
Kentucky, 76
Kerens, Richard C., 111-112
Kidwell, Dr. Thomas L., 84-85
Kingsbury, John M., 72-75

LAC Minerals USA, 118, 131-138
La Ciénega, 4, 87
LA number, 42, 123, 129
La Turquesa, 125
Ladron de Guevara, Ygnacio, 43, 45
Lamy (town), 108
Lamy, Bishop, 76
Lane, Governor, 64, 76
Langham, Juan (John), 51
Las Cruces, 105
Las Norias, 62, 92, 93, 96, 129
Las Norias Mines Co., 124
Las Vegas, 56
Laughlin, Ruth, 31
Lawson, W. T., 118, 120
lead glaze (pottery), 15
Leadville, Colorado, 102, 106
Leitensdorfer, Juan Eugenio, 70-75, 86
Lewis, Capt. Meriwether, 7
Lexington, Missouri, 104
Lone Mountain, 3
Lone Mountain Ranch, 128
Lopez, Damaso, 36, 39, 41-43, 45-46, 50-51, 53, 65
Lordsburg, 89
Los Alamos (county), 107
Los Angeles Times, 104
Lovato, Luís, 6, 8, 12, 35, 37, 43
Lower Mill, 94, 96, 129
Lowe's Missouri Battery, 104

Lukas (Lucas) Canyon, 6, 133
Lummis, Charles, 34, 58, 101, 104

Madrid, 80, 87-88, 95, 104, 111-112, 118, 125
Madrid Siding, 112
Madrid Tract, 109-112
magistral, 22
magnetite, 20-21, 119
manta, 32-33
manto, 33
Manzanos, 56
Marsh, Mary Wayne (Mae), 112
Martín, Diego, 51-53
Martinez, Ben, 126
Martinez, Carlos, 126
Martinez de Montoya, Juan, 16
Martinez, Fray Damian, 18
Mary's Bar, 108
masa, 22
Maxwell Land Grant, 103, 105-106
McCormick, R. C., 82
McDonald, W. L., 128
McKinnis, Charles, 124
McKnight, John, 27
McLaughlin, J. T., 6
McPhee shaft, 90-91, 115
Medina, Bartolomé de, 22
Meiklejohn, Doug, 135
mercury, 18, 21-22, 47, 63, 110
Meriwether, David, 7, 25
Mesilla, 102
Mexican National Congress, 50
Mexico City, 25-26
Mexico, Republic of, 4, 12, 25-27, 61
Miami, Oklahoma, 128
Miller, John, 118-121, 125
Miller, N. M., 68-69, 77, 85
Millington, D. A., 108
mina, 17, 23, 40, 42
mineral rights, 44
Mining Deputation, 36
Mining Tribunal, 57
Mining World, 121
Missouri, 26, 28-30, 82, 102, 104
Missouri-Kansas Syndicate, 116
Missouri River,
Moebius and Thum Balbach, 110
mojonera, 23
molienda, 46

Montana, Art, 136-137
Monte Largo, 4
Monterrey, Viceroy, 15
Montoya, Guadalupe, 113
Montoya, Maraquita, 40, 64-66
Montoya Federal Building, 53
Moreno Water & Mining Company, 89
Morfi, 18
mortero de minas, 17
muller stones, 47

negro (mineral), 20
New Jersey, 118-121
New Live Oak mine (claim), 48, 128
New Mexico & Southern Pacific R. R., 107, 108
New Mexico Environment Department, 134, 136
New Mexico Environmental Law Center, 135
New Mexico School of Mines, 121
New Mexico Territorial Council,
New Placer, 3, 11, 32, 49, 58-61, 104-105, 108-109, 122, 124
New Spain, 18, 22, 25, 27, 48
New York (state or city), 69, 104, 105-106, 110, 117, 129
New York & New Mexico Mining & Smelting Co., 108
North Carolina, 36, 67
Nuestra Señora de los Dolores, 8, 23, 113, 123
Nuestra Señora de los Reyes de Linares, 16-17
Nuevas Leyes y Ordenanzas, 36

O'Bannon, Andrew J., 75, 77
O'Donojú, Viceroy Juan, 25
Ohio, 67, 102
Ojo Caliente, 51
Ojo del Oso, 8, 34, 136
ojito de carbon Piedra, 87
Old Ortiz Mine, 5, 42, 53, 62, 68, 93, 93, 115, 120, 124, 131, 133
Old Placer, 32, 55, 58-59, 108, 122
Old Timer Creek, 59
Oñate, Juan de, 15
Ordenanzas de Minería, 11, 36, 63, 78
Ordenanzas del Nuevo Cuaderno, 36

Oro (settlement), 12, 19-20, 23-24, 35, 43, 58
Oro, Sierra del, 23-24
Ortiz (settlement), 107
Ortiz Cooperative Livestock Association, 128
Ortiz, Francisco, 39, 45, 52
Ortiz Gold King Mining Company, 124
Ortiz Joint Venture, 133
Ortiz, José Francisco, 35, 38-46, 49-53, 55, 64, 77, 110, 130, 139
Ortiz Mines Company, 128-129, 130-133
Ortiz Mine Syndicate, 124
Ortiz Porphyry Belt, 4
Ortiz Ranch, 40
Ortiz, Rosendo, 125-126
Ortiz, Rumaldo, 126
Oso, Sierra del, 23-24, 65
Oso Spring, 12, 23, 35, 43-44, 71, 79, 89, 123
Otero, Jose Antonio, 76
Otero, Michael (Miguel) A., 75-76
Otero, Miguel (Gillie) A. Jr., 76, 106, 114
Owen, Richard E., 83

Pachuca, 22
Padre Mina, 32, 139
Palace Avenue, 24
Palace Hotel (Cerrillos), 129
Palace of the Governors, 7, 16
Pareje de las Norias, 51
Parker, Charles G., 85, 88
Parker, Tom, 135
Parral, 16
patio, 10, 22
Patio Amalgamation Process, 22, 48
patria chica, 53
Pecos and Placer Mining and Ditch Company, 84
Pecos Pueblo, 3
Pecos Pueblo Land Grant, 75
Pecos River, 83-84, 89, 109
Pegasus Gold Corporation, 133-135
Pennsylvania, 96
Peñuela, Governor, 16
pepena, 11, 32
Perea, Ben, 126
Perea, Teddy, 126
Perez, Albino, 53
Peticolas, Sgt. Alfred B., 81

pica, 10, 19
piedras de moler, 47
Pike, Zebulon, 25
Pilar Quiroa, Ana María, 50
piloncillo, 54
Pino, Pedro Bautista, 28
Placer Dome, 134
Placer Mountains, 64, 86
placer nuevo, 58, 60
placer viejo, 58, 60
porphyry, monzonite, 4
Porter, Earl, 73
Portugal, 67
Potter, George W., 128
Potter, Mrs. George W. (Emily W.), 128
Potter-Simms Laboratory, 129
Prada, Fray Juan de, 16
pregnant solution, 132
Puleston, Col., 82
pyrites, 99, 133

quicksilver, 10, 22, 47, 63, 97-98

Ramirez Hacienda, 86
Raymond, R.W., 33, 99
Real de Aguilar, Capt. Alfonso, 16-17, 87
reale (coin), 39, 45
Red River, 89
Rencher, Abraham, 67-69, 72-75, 77-79, 86, 99
Rencher, W.C., 99
retort, 22, 47
reverse osmosis, 133, 136
Rio Arriba, 51
Rio Grande, 7
Risque, Ferdinand W., 75, 77
Rivera, Brigadier Don Pedro de, 18
Riverside, 57
Roberson, Paul, 130
Roberts, William H., 100
Robidoux (Robidú), Antonio, 45, 56
Rocky Mountains, 72, 75, 96
Rodriguez, Fray Agustín, 15
Roosevelt, President, 125
Rosario, 107
Royal Fifth, 11, 24
Roybal, Vicar Santiago, 4
Rubidoux, California (city), 57
Ruelena, mina de, 37

- 152 -

Ruelle, Jean Baptiste, 57
St. Louis, 70, 86, 112
St. Louis Democrat, 86
Salazar, Juan Damaso, 45
Salinas, 16
Sandía, 16
San Bernardino, 57
San Buenaventura, 16
San Fernando Mission, 57
San Francisco, Real de, 95
San Juan, 51
San Ildefonso, 55
San Lázaro Pueblo, 2, 23
San Lázaro, Sierra de, 17, 19, 23-24
San Lazarus Creek, 59
San Luís Potosí, 8, 48
San Marcos, Arroyo, 87
San Marcos Pueblo, 2, 16, 23
San Marcos, Sierra de, 15, 23
San Marcos spring, 95
San Pedro (settlement), 3, 58, 83, 114, 125
San Pedro and Cañon del Agua Mining Company, 86, 108
San Pedro Mountains, 4, 17, 19, 23, 37, 58-59
Sanchez, Esmeregildo, 53
Sandia Mining Company, 111
Sandoval (county), 107
Sandoval, A., 126
Sandoval, Frank, 126
Santa Fe Botanical Garden, 136, 138-139
Santa Fe Democrat, 99
Santa Fe Plaza, 3, 14, 24
Santa Fe Ring, 103, 105
Santa Fe, Rio, 73
Santa Fe Trail, 4, 26-27, 29-30, 53, 60, 70
Santa Fe Trust for Public Lands, 136
Santa Fe Weekly Gazette, 83
Santa Rosa, 75
Santa Rosa, mina de, 37
Santa Rosalia (mine), 39, 42-46, 49-51, 53-54, 65, 67, 78, 85, 111
Santa Rosalia Mine Grant, 40, 50-51, 78
Santo Domingo, 55
Santo Niño, la mina del, 8-9, 12-13, 35, 37-38, 41-46, 53, 56-57, 64-65, 85, 91, 111, 124, 138
sapphires, 15
sawmill, 85

Schmitt, Frank, 118
Seguro, Cerro, 4
sheep, 54-55, 116
Sherman, Charles E., 75, 77
Shoshone lode, 122
Sibley, General, 81
Silas Mason Company, 129
Silver City, 36
Silver Purchase Act of 1934, 125
Silver Purchasing Act of 1890, 112
Simms, Frank, 128
Smith, Jedediah, 27, 30
Spanish Cortes, 28
Springer, Frank, 103
Sonora, 24, 27, 40
South Africa, 131
South Mountain, 4
squatters, 112
Staley, David P., 20, 99
stamp mill, 21, 48, 70-72, 78-79, 84-86, 88, 98-99, 101, 108
Steck, Dr. Michael, 64, 70, 84-89, 92-99
Strickland, Superintendent, 115
Suma Indians, 16
surface rights, 44, 126
Surveyor General, 64, 66, 76-78
Sweet, Irving, 118

tahona, 21, 46-48, 71
tanate, 10, 32
Tanoan, 23
Taos, 29
Tertiary intrusive, 4, 6
Tewa, 55
Texas, 26, 39, 89
Thornton, 107
tienda, 55, 130
Tijeras, 56
Tiro, mina de, 37
Tiwa, 16
Tompiro, 16
Torrance (county), 107
Tournier, Jean Baptiste, 36, 56, 62
Towa, 3
Townley, 40, 46, 83, 86
Townsend's big-eared bat, 13, 138
Treaty of Córdova, 25
Treaty of Guadalupe Hidalgo, 66, 78
trespass miners, 86
Tuerto, Arroyo del, 6, 58-59

- 153 -

Tuerto, El (settlement), 16, 86
Tuerto Mountains, El, 17
Tules, La Doña, 24-25, 55, 60
Tunia (shaft), 12, 44, 85, 90-91, 138

U.S. Farm Security Administration, 128
United States Marshal, 56
U.S. mining law, 61, 63
U.S. Post Office, 100
Universal Placer Mining Company, 121, 125

Valencia, 76
vara, (measure) 8, 25, 40, (in leagues) 42-43, 45, 57, 65-66
Varela, Mariano, 57
Vicente de la Ciénaga, 36
Vicksburg, 82, 104
Viejo, Arroyo, 6, 44, 118, 120
Vigil y Alarid, Juan Bautista, 24
Virginia, 76

Waldo (station), 107, 112
Walker, David, 75
Walker, Joel P., 28
Walker, Thomas J., 77
Wallace, Lew, 106
War Board Order L-208, 126
Ward, Ulysses, 75
Warren, A. Helene, 2
Washington City, 68-69
Watrous, Sam, 55-56, 62
Watts, John S., 83
Webb, James Josiah, 72, 75
West Virginia, 104-105, 110, 117
Westport, 72-73
Whatnot Shop, 108
Wheeler Survey, 95
whim, 42
Whittlesey, Elisha, 64, 67, 75, 77
Wilbar, W., 76
Willing, George M., 83
windlass, 11, 33, 59
Wislizenus, Dr., 55, 57, 61
Wolf, Alfred, 100
Wolf, Doug, 135-136
World War II, 126
Wright, Daniel, 84, 87

Young, Frank, 126

Zacatecas, 48
Zaldivar, Vicente de, 15, 17, 22, 72
zinc, 21, 109, 132